RESOURCES FOR THE FUTURE LIBRARY COLLECTION
ENERGY POLICY

Volume 6

The Leasing of Federal Lands for Fossil Fuels Production

Full list of titles in the set
ENERGY POLICY

The Leasing of Federal Lands for Fossil Fuels Production

Stephen L. McDonald

Washington, DC • London

Publisher's note

The publisher has made every effort to ensure the quality of this reprint, but points out that some imperfections in the original copies may be apparent.

At Earthscan we strive to minimize our environmental impacts and carbon footprint through reducing waste, recycling and offsetting our CO_2 emissions, including those created through publication of this book. For more details of our environmental policy, see www.earthscan.co.uk.

The Leasing of Federal Lands for Fossil Fuels Production

The Leasing of Federal Lands for Fossil Fuels Production

Stephen L. McDonald

Published for Resources for the Future
By The Johns Hopkins University Press
Baltimore and London

This book is a product of the Center for Energy Policy Research under the
co-direction of Hans H. Landsberg and Sam H. Schurr. Stephen L. McDonald is
professor of economics at the University of Texas at Austin.

The book was edited by Jo Hinkel. The illustrations were prepared by Federal
Graphics. The index was prepared by Toni Warner.

RFF editors: Joan R. Tron, Ruth B. Haas, Jo Hinkel, Sally A. Skillings

Contents

List of Figures

Acknowledgments

In an undertaking of this sort a researcher-author becomes indebted to many people for help of one kind or another. I should like to acknowledge my indebtedness and offer my sincere thanks to the following persons.

For their help in connection with my research, I thank Alton K. Cavin, Robert R. Wilson, J. B. Lowenhaupt, John Rankin, H. Roy McBroom, N. O. Frederick, A. Dewey Acuff, Jack Hendricks, J. Rogers Pearcy, John M. Meier, Lowell G. Hammons, Harry McAndrews, Gary Bennethum, William Moffat, Darius W. Gaskins, Collis P. Chandler, Bob Burch, and Milton Lipton.

My thanks go also to those who read earlier versions of the manuscript and made helpful comments: James W. McKie, Herbert H. Liebhafsky, Hermann Enzer, William A. Vogely, Robert Adams, Robert J. Kalter, Wallace E. Tyner, Patrick H. Geehan, Hans H. Landsberg, John J. Schanz, Walter J. Mead, Carl C. Traywick, Vincent J. Geraci, and George Heitmann.

If, despite all this help, errors remain in the manuscript, I alone am responsible for them.

Finally, I am most grateful to Resources for the Future for their generous grant which made this work possible.

Austin, Texas   Stephen L. McDonald

Foreword

The federal government's ownership of offshore and onshore lands bearing coal, oil, and gas gives it a dominating role in future domestic energy supply. Some may welcome this, others deplore it, but neither attitude will alter the importance to the economy of the terms and the pace of the federal government's leasing of its fossil fuel resources.

The concern with federal land leasing is not, of course, new. Without going back into more remote history, it is probably fair to say that the formation of the Public Land Law Review Commission in 1965 marked the beginning of what has proved to be an extended period of escalating interest in assuring "that the public lands of the United States shall be (a) retained and managed or (b) disposed of, all in a manner to provide the maximum benefit for the general public." While the commission report may not have stimulated as much response as intended, the management of federal leases for the production of oil and gas from the outer continental shelf or the onshore production of western coal and oil shale has attracted the attention of a large number of federal employees charged with management responsibilities for retained lands. In addition, a number of resource scholars have been intrigued by an opportunity to study an interesting array of complex resource allocation and distribution issues.

The manner and pace in which government develops publicly owned fuel resources affects the energy supply stream from both public and private lands, the behavior of the energy marketplace, how well we are able to deal with the problem of threatening energy shortages, and what price levels might be called for to cope with them. Simultaneously, there is the necessary consideration of the public's sharing in the resource values being severed from the land as well as in bearing the burden of uncertainty. The proper balancing of rewards and risks is a delicate task.

No single volume can examine fully the many questions involved: among them, whether to retain or dispose, to lease now or later, to favor royalties or bonuses, to control or not control rates of production, or how to choose among the various standards of engineering efficiency and economic efficiency. The late seventies finds the country in the midst of a vast federal effort to make decisions of this kind. Even though the evolution of a new federal leasing policy seems to be advancing at too slow a speed to be geared into energy policy more generally, the pace of events is moving too swiftly to write and publish books on the specifics of the contemporary policies being formulated and the procedures being established. Yet, those entering this arena have need to acquire a basic understanding of what basic goals and practices are involved.

Stephen McDonald's book admirably fills this need. RFF has turned to him before, always to illuminate an area in which theory blends into practice, or rather where practice needs to be analyzed in the light of theory. *Petroleum Conservation in the United States: An Economic Analysis,* published in 1971, gave him a chance to study petroleum production practices, above all the important matter of unitized field control. In 1974 he contributed an essay on "Incentives in Energy Production and Consumption: A Research Agenda" to a volume RFF published under the title of *Energy and the Social Sciences;* and later on he contributed the background paper on maximum efficient recovery (MER) that formed the basis of an RFF workshop on this important and controversial tool of petroleum supply management. We are delighted once again to have assisted in making his insights available to a broader audience.

Hans H. Landsberg, Co-Director
Center for Energy Policy Research

August 1978

The Leasing of Federal Lands for Fossil Fuels Production

1

Introduction

This study was undertaken on the premise that the greater part of the nation's remaining fossil fuel resources are to be found on lands, offshore and onshore, under federal jurisdiction, and that the procedures, terms, and conditions under which these lands are leased for minerals production will significantly affect the nation's energy economy for many years to come. It has been recently estimated that about two-thirds of our remaining oil resources and 40 percent of our remaining natural gas resources are located on the outer continental shelf. About 40 percent of the country's known coal resources are situated on federal lands in the West. About three-fourths of the acreage containing oil shale deposits with commercial potential consists of public lands.[1] All these lands are leased, or are subject to lease by the Department of the Interior, to private operators under procedures, terms, and conditions prescribed by federal statutes and regulations. In view of the nation's energy problems and prospects, the question may be raised whether existing leasing practices and associated regulation of lessee operations contribute what they could to an efficient energy economy. We shall try to give at least a tentative answer to that question.

The granting of mineral leases on federal lands is administered by the Bureau of Land Management (BLM) of the Department of the In-

---

[1] Statement of Harrison Loesch in *Federal Leasing and Disposal Policies,* Hearings before the Senate Committee on Interior and Insular Affairs (Washington, D.C., June 19, 1972) pp. 35–37. A more recent (1975) estimate of oil and gas resources by the U.S. Geological Survey assigns about a third of these resources to the outer continental shelf. For various estimates, see Robert J. Kalter, Wallace E. Tyner, and Daniel W. Hughes, *Alternative Energy Leasing Strategies and Schedules for the Outer Continental Shelf* (Ithaca, N.Y., Cornell University, 1975) pp. 9–10.

terior, with some technical assistance regarding geological features and probable value from the Geological Survey of the Department of the Interior. The supervision of lessees, including environmental and conservation regulation, is primarily the responsibility of the Geological Survey.[2] Except for certain leases for oil and gas production on onshore federal lands, leases are granted to the operator bidding the highest lease bonus (if it is deemed acceptable), with rental and royalty rates specified in the lease offer. Onshore oil and gas leases of lands not on a known geological structure of a producing field are granted to the first qualified applicant for a $10 filing fee, with rental and royalty rates specified.

As the law is officially interpreted, the major objectives in the management of publicly owned mineral resources are "(1) to assure orderly and timely resource development; (2) to protect the environment; (3) to insure the public a fair market value return on the disposition of its resources."[3] No one of these objectives dominates the others, and it is not clear from the law or official pronouncements how they are to be reconciled if they conflict in application, as they may. For instance, sufficiently strong measures to protect the environment may delay development and may also reduce the value of resources to prospective lessees. Or sufficiently rapid development may result in less than fair market value being received. It is, in any case, not clear just what "orderly and timely" development means in practice. On the other hand, these three objectives may be mutually consistent if we can integrate them into one decision rule, as we try to do in this study.

Basically, our argument is this: the Department of the Interior should try to capture a maximum of the present value of the pure economic rent arising from minerals production on federal lands, where *pure economic rent* is the income which tends to accrue in the long run, under conditions of perfect competition and the absence of externalities, to the owners of raw natural resources. This rule, as we shall try to show, is the equivalent of the rule that the Department of the Interior should try to maximize the value of natural resources to society.

---

[2] The act establishing a new Department of Energy in the federal government (Public Law 95-91, August 4, 1977) transfers to the secretary of the new department certain powers formerly exercised by the BLM and the Geological Survey. These include the promulgation of regulations to foster competition in the bidding for federal leases, to implement alternative bidding systems, to establish diligence requirements, and to set rates of production (ibid., sec. 302b).

[3] Loesch, *Federal Leasing and Disposal Policies*, p. 38.

We do not mean to suggest that the department attempt to measure, a priori, the pure economic rent available and then insist upon using the figure as a minimum payment by the lessee; there is no practical way it can do that. Rather, we mean to say that the Department of the Interior should try to create and maintain leasing conditions which are conducive to the desired result. Thus, for example, conditions that reduce lessee uncertainty, that increase effective competition for leases, that increase efficiency of resource extraction, that internalize externalities such as environmental damage—all these and perhaps others tend to result in Interior's capturing a maximum of the pure economic rent available.

In this study our rule does three things. First, it allows us to integrate the three objectives listed on page 2. It tells us at once what "fair market value" should mean, how environmental controls properly contribute to it, and how, by reducing rent to present value, we can give definite meaning to "orderly and timely development." Second, it allows us to show the relevance of the conservation and related regulation imposed by the Geological Survey on lessees to the objective of obtaining fair market value. With particular reference to oil and gas on the outer continental shelf, we can outline the appropriate approach to regulation. Third, it provides a criterion by which to evaluate some features of the leasing process, such as bonus bidding, and some alternatives, such as royalty bidding. In essence this study consists of the application of our rule to the analysis of all major features of the leasing process and its possible alternatives.

There are at least two things we do not try to do. First, we do not concern ourselves with administrative or procedural details. We do not attempt, for instance, to say how and when notices of lease sales should be published. We do not concern ourselves with the problem, which operators naturally complain of, of excessive red tape in leasing and related regulation. Second, we attempt no quantitative modeling. We do not attempt to say that the Department of the Interior should lease some specific number of acres per year, or that it would receive some specific number of additional dollars per year if it changed some procedure. The latter sort of thing is, no doubt, important, but it is beyond the scope of this study.[4]

---

[4] The author has been particularly impressed by the modeling work of Kalter and coauthors, *Alternative Energy Leasing Strategies*.

It should be noted that not all minerals found on federal lands are subject to the leasing laws. The so-called hard-rock minerals, including uranium, are subject to the location and claim system of establishing production rights. We exclude them from this discussion, of course. We further narrow the discussion to those leasable minerals that are pertinent to the energy problem—oil and gas, and coal and oil shale. While much of what we have to say is relevant to such leasable minerals as sulfur, phosphates, sodium, and potassium, we do not attempt to deal with the problems and issues that may be uniquely pertinent to them.

It will be observed by the reader that rather more space is given to oil and gas than to coal and oil shale. The reason for this is the fact that oil and gas present a unique regulatory problem, that of conservation, which is extremely important to the results of leasing. This problem, which is little understood by the general public, must be discussed at some length; hence the additional space given to oil and gas leasing and related practices.

In chapter 2 we will begin with the legal basis of leasing practice, citing the relevant statutes and regulations. Our purpose is not simply to say what the law is, important as that may be, but rather to outline and explain actual practices. Chapters 3 and 4 are theoretical; in them we will develop the analytical framework. In chapter 3 we will discuss in detail the nature and determinants of economic rent, will define for our purposes "pure economic rent," and will show that maximizing pure economic rent is the equivalent of maximizing the value of natural resources to society. Chapter 4 is devoted to the problem of the optimum rate of output of minerals, with specific reference to oil and gas, and to the economics of environmental protection. We will show the relevance of efficient extraction and environmental protection to maximizing pure economic rent.

Having developed the analytical framework, we devote the next four chapters to the analysis of specific procedures in land leasing. Chapter 5 is concerned with the manner and rate of land leasing. Here we will try to show that leasing should be on the basis of competitive bidding, and that, under some circumstances, accelerated leasing may be in the interest of maximizing the present value of pure economic rent. In Chapter 6 we take up alternative bidding systems—bonus bidding, royalty bidding, profit-share bidding, and other combinations. We also consider sequential bidding, installment-bonus payment, and working-interest bidding. Chapter 5 is concerned with production (conservation) regulation, with particular reference to oil and gas production on the outer continental shelf. An argument is made for the compulsory unitization of reservoirs with operator freedom as to well spacing and production rate, although we do recognize that there is considerable merit in regulation on the basis of the maximum efficient rate (MER) with explicit economic content. Chapter 8 is devoted to the subject of environmental regulation. We will argue that the objective should be internalization of actual environmental costs and not absolute environmental protection, but we find difficulties associated with the measurement of environmental costs. Chapter 9 contains a summary of our conclusions and recommendations.

2

The Legal Basis of Leasing Practice

To begin, we will review the statutes and regulations governing the leasing of federal lands. Such a review will indicate not only the legal foundations but also the nature of actual practice. Incidentally, it will also provide the basis for later indicating whether changes in the law would be required to authorize certain changes in practice that have been or may be suggested. We will make no attempt in this review to cover every detail of law; rather, our purpose will be to bring out those major features which have a bearing on the largely economic analysis that constitutes the bulk of this study.

The presentation is organized by statutes, but at appropriate points we will provide the content of major amplifying regulations. We will ignore those regulations that merely repeat statutory provisions, or those that concern administrative details of no particular relevance to our study. Also, at this time we will not discuss operating regulations governing lessees; these will be taken up at a later point in the context of efficiency, conservation, and related matters.

THE MINERAL LEASING ACT OF 1920, AS AMENDED

GENERAL CONSIDERATIONS

The Mineral Leasing Act of 1920 is the basic law governing the leasing of onshore public lands (as distinguished from the outer continental shelf, covered by another statute).[1] The act provides that

> . . . Deposits of coal, phosphate, sodium, potassium, oil, oil shale, native asphalt, solid and semisolid bitumen, and bituminous rock, . . . or gas,

[1] 30 U.S.C. 181–287.

6

and lands containing such deposits owned by the United States [with certain exceptions] shall be subject to disposition in the form and manner provided [hereinafter] to citizens of the United States, or to associations of such citizens, or to any corporation organized under the laws of the United States, or to any State or Territory thereof, or in the case of coal, oil, oil shale, or gas, to municipalities.[2]

The United States reserves rights to helium.[3] The provisions of the act apply also to deposits of the minerals enumerated above in such lands as may have been or may be disposed of under laws reserving mineral rights to the United States.[4]

The leases or permits which a person, association, or corporation may own or control at any one time are limited. In the case of coal, the limit is 46,080 acres in any one state, and 100,000 acres in the United States as a whole.[5] In the case of oil and gas the limit is 246,080 acres in any one state other than Alaska, where the limit is 300,000 acres in each of the northern and southern leasing districts. Options to acquire oil and gas leases are also limited to 200,000 acres in any one state other than Alaska, and to 200,000 acres in each of the Alaskan leasing districts.[6]

Any state owning lands acquired from the United States may consent to the development and operation of such lands under agreements approved by the secretary of the interior for the purpose of conserving oil and gas resources, including agreements for cooperative or unit development and operation of oil or gas pools, fields, or areas.[7]

Each federal lease must contain provisions for the exercise of reasonable diligence, skill, and care in operations, for the safety and welfare of miners, and for the prevention of undue wastes.[8] A lease may be forfeited or canceled by an appropriate proceeding in a U.S. district court whenever the lessee fails to comply with lease provisions or regulations.[9]

[2] 20 U.S.C. 181. We shall be concerned only with oil and gas, coal, and oil shale.

[3] Ibid.

[4] 30 U.S.C. 182.

[5] 30 U.S.C. 184(a)(1).

[6] 30 U.S.C. 184d.

[7] 30 U.S.C. 184a. Under a unit agreement, the operators in a common reservoir pool their interests, share revenues and costs by formula, and appoint a manager to operate the reservoir as a unit. This approach to oil and gas conservation will be discussed in detail at a later point in this study.

[8] 30 U.S.C. 187.

[9] 30 U.S.C. 188.

The secretary of the interior is authorized to prescribe rules and regulations necessary to effect the purposes of the act. Nothing in the act may be construed as affecting the rights of states, including the right to collect taxes on improvements, output, or other assets of a lessee of the United States.[10]

All money received for sales, bonuses, royalties, and rentals of public lands affected by the act shall be paid into the Treasury of the United States. However, the Treasury shall periodically pay 50 percent of such receipts to the state in which the pertinent lands are located. These funds are to be used at the direction of the legislature, with priority being given to areas impacted by mineral development, for planning, construction, and maintenance of public facilities, and provision of public service. Further, except in the case of Alaska, 40 percent of receipts shall be paid into the reclamation fund. In the case of Alaska, 90 percent of the receipts shall be put at the disposal of the legislature.[11]

Oil and gas royalties are payable in kind; the secretary is authorized to sell such proceeds on sealed bids or at public auction, and, in some circumstances, to sell them at private sale at the market price or to accept their value from the lessee.[12]

COAL

With specific reference to coal, the secretary of the interior is authorized to divide lands into leasing tracts of appropriate size. From time to time the secretary is empowered to offer such lands for leasing, and awards are to be made on the basis of competitive bidding. No less than 50 percent of the acreage offered in any one year shall be leased under a system of deferred bonus payment. No bid shall be accepted if it represents less than fair market value, as determined by the secretary. No lease sale shall be held unless the coal lands have been included in a comprehensive land use plan and the sale is compatible with the plan.[13] The secretary may issue to any person an exploration license, but such license shall confer no right to a lease.[14]

[10] 30 U.S.C. 189.
[11] 30 U.S.C. 191.
[12] 30 U.S.C. 192.
[13] 30 U.S.C. 201(a).
[14] 30 U.S.C. 201(b).

The secretary, upon determining that maximum economic recovery of coal is served thereby, may approve the consolidation of coal leases into a logical mining unit, such unit being defined as an area in which coal resources can be developed in an efficient, economical, and orderly manner as a unit. After establishment of a logical mining unit, the reserves must be mined out within a period of time set by the secretary but not for more than forty years.[15]

Coal leases shall be operative for a term of twenty years and so long thereafter as coal is produced in commercial quantities from respective leases. The secretary shall regulate annual rentals on leases. Royalty on production shall be not less than 12½ percent of the value of produced coal, except that the secretary may set a lower rate on coal recovered by underground mining methods. Rentals and royalties are subject to readjustment at the end of twenty years and at the end of each subsequent ten-year period.[16]

Prior to taking action on a lease that might significantly disturb the environment, the lessee must submit, for the secretary's approval, an operation and reclamation plan.[17]

The secretary is authorized and directed to conduct a comprehensive exploratory program in order to obtain sufficient data to evaluate the extent, location, and potential for development of coal resources subject to leasing. The activities authorized include seismic, geophysical, geochemical, and stratigraphic drilling explorations.[18] This provision does not limit the rights of private persons to conduct similar exploratory activities.[19] The secretary shall make available to the public all data, maps, interpretations, and so forth, acquired in the exploration activities so authorized.[20]

SOME AMPLIFYING COAL REGULATIONS

Tracts proposed for leasing are to be selected by the Bureau of Land Management (BLM) and the Geological Survey field offices, with participation by affected state governments and other surface-management

[15] 30 U.S.C. 201(d).
[16] 30 U.S.C. 207(a).
[17] 30 U.S.C. 207(c).
[18] 30 U.S.C. 208A(a).
[19] 30 U.S.C. 208A(b).
[20] 30 U.S.C. 208A(d).

agencies, on the basis of relevant information included in the appropriate land use plan, in nominations, and in competitive coal lease applications on file. Factors to be considered in selection include the depth, quality, thickness, and extent of the coal resource; the availability of water; the relationship of the coal to existing communities; the potential impact of coal production on local economies; the availability of service and access corridors; esthetic qualities; and rehabilitation potential of the land.[21]

Prior to each lease sale, the authorized officer of the BLM shall publish a notice of the proposed sale in the *Federal Register* and in at least one newspaper of general circulation in the affected county. The notice must include, among other things, the time and place of sale, whether the sale will be by sealed bids or public auction, a description of the land, and an indication of the place where a more detailed statement of terms and conditions may be obtained.[22]

Also before the lease sale, the Geological Survey, "considering public comments on fair market value and available geotechnical, engineering and economic data, shall make a coal resource economic evaluation of each tract to be sold and shall submit it to the authorized officer [of the BLM]."[23]

As for the sale itself, the regulations state that:

Bids will be received only until the hour on the date specified in the notice of competitive leasing. All bids submitted after the hour will be rejected. The authorized officer will read all sealed bids. If the procedure calls for sealed bids followed by oral bids the oral bidding will begin at the level of the highest sealed bid received. After the oral bidding has ceased, the highest bid will be announced. . . . [However] no decision to accept or reject any bid will be made at this time. The sale will be adjourned and the sale panel will convene to determine if the bid adequately reflects fair market value considering, among other factors, comments on fair market value. The recommendations of the panel will be sent to the authorized officer, who . . . will make the final decision to accept a bid or reject all bids, as soon as possible after the sale date. The successful bidder will be notified in writing. The Department reserves the right to reject any and all bids but will not accept any bids which are less than the fair market value of the tract.[24]

[21] 43 CFR 3525.3(b).
[22] 43 CFR 3525.15(g).
[23] 43 CFR 3525.17(a).
[24] 43 CFR 3525.17(b).

OIL AND GAS

To return to the Mineral Leasing Act itself, the secretary may lease such lands covered by the act as are known or believed to contain oil or gas. If the lands are within any known geological structure of a producing oil or gas field, they shall be leased by competitive bidding in units of not more than 640 acres upon payment of an acceptable bonus, with obligation of the lessee to pay a royalty on production specified in the lease, but not less than 12½ percent of the amount or value of production removed or sold. If the lands are not within a known geological structure of a producing field, they shall be leased to the first qualified applicant with provision for a royalty of 12½ percent of production removed or sold. All leases are conditioned upon payment of a rental of not less than 50 cents per acre per year, due in advance. However, a minimum royalty of $1 per acre in lieu of rental shall be paid at the end of each year following the discovery of oil or gas in paying quantities.[25]

Competitive leases shall be granted for a primary term of five years; with noncompetitive leases having a term of ten years. Leases shall continue, however, so long as oil or gas is produced in paying quantities. The primary term must be extended for two years if drilling operations are commenced and diligently prosecuted on the lease, or on a unitized area embracing the lease, before the expiration of the primary term.[26] If, in his opinion, lands of the United States are being drained by oil or gas wells on adjacent land, the secretary may negotiate agreements or compensate the United States and its lessees, with the consent of the latter, and leases on the affected land shall be extended so long as compensation is paid plus one year.[27]

For the purpose of conserving oil or gas, lessees may unite with each other in collectively adopting and operating under a cooperative or unit plan for a pool, field, or like area, or any part thereof, whenever such plan is determined and certified by the secretary to be in the public interest: "The Secretary may provide that oil and gas leases hereafter issued under [the relevant sections] of this title shall contain a provision requiring the lessee to operate under such a reasonable cooperative or

[25] 30 U.S.C. 226(a)–(d).
[26] 30 U.S.C. 226(e).
[27] 30 U.S.C. 226(g).

unit plan, and he may prescribe such a plan under which such lessee shall operate, which shall adequately protect the rights of all parties in interest, including the United States."[28] An approved plan may contain a provision under which the secretary, or any person, committee, or state, or federal officer, or agency is authorized to alter the rate of prospecting, development, or production under the plan. Leases operated under an approved cooperative or unit plan shall be excepted in determining acreage held subject to quantitative limitations. Leases may be pooled to form drilling units in conformity with an established well-spacing or development program.[29]

Some Amplifying Oil and Gas Regulations

It is the responsibility of the director of the Geological Survey to determine the boundaries of the known geological structures of producing oil and gas fields, to publish notification of determinations made in the *Federal Register,* and to file in the proper office maps or diagrams showing structural boundaries.[30]

Leases or applications for leases committed to an approved unit or cooperative plan shall not be included in computing accountable acreage.[31] The amount of acquired lands acreage that may be held under lease may not be in excess of the allowable amount of public domain acreage. That is, "Public domain lease holdings shall not be charged against acquired lands lease holdings; such respective holdings shall not be interchargeable."[32]

Offers for noncompetitive oil and gas leases must be accompanied by a filing fee of $10 for each offer, plus the full payment of the first year's rental. The filing fee is retained, even when the offer is withdrawn or rejected. Rentals are payable in advance at rates of 50 cents per acre on noncompetitive leases located outside a known geological structure of a producing field; at rates of $2 per acre on such leases after determination that they are located inside a structure; and $2 per acre on competitive leases prior to a discovery, unless a different rate is

[28] 30 U.S.C. 226(j).
[29] Ibid.
[30] 43 CFR 3100.7-1–3100.7-2.
[31] 43 CFR 3101.1-5.
[32] 43 CFR 3101.2-4.

prescribed in the lease. On noncompetitive leases, royalty rates shall be 12½ percent; on competitive leases, they shall be as prescribed in the notice of sale; and on certain exchange and renewal leases, they shall be graduated rates related to daily oil and gas production.[33]

In order to maximize ultimate recovery of oil and gas and to conserve these resources, the secretary may waive, suspend, or reduce rental or royalty rates whenever he determines it necessary to promote development or allow economical operation of leases.[34]

Applications to unitize oil or gas fields must be filed with the regional oil and gas supervisor of the Geological Survey. In order to be approved by the secretary, unitization agreements must be made for the purpose of conserving oil or gas and must be certified by the secretary as necessary or advisable in the public interest. The secretary is authorized to approve communitization or drilling agreements when separate tracts cannot be independently developed and operated in conformance with an established well-spacing or development program. The secretary may also approve combinations of lessee interests for the purpose of constructing and operating refineries, pipelines, and railroad lines to handle oil or gas produced on lessees' lands. Finally, to avoid waste or promote conservation, he may approve the subsurface storage of oil or gas on federal lands.[35]

Noncompetitive Oil and Gas Leases. The regulation states, "All noncompetitive leases shall be for a primary term of 10 years and so long thereafter as oil or gas is produced in paying quantities."[36] An offer to lease may not include more than 2,560 acres, nor less than 640 acres except where the lands affected are in an approved cooperative or unit plan of operation. An offer may be withdrawn if notice is received in the proper office before the lease is signed on behalf of the United States, or in the case of a simultaneous offer, before the drawing (see below). If more than one offer to lease acreage covered by an expired, canceled, relinquished, or terminated lease is filed during the stated period, the offers shall be considered simultaneous and their priorities determined by a public drawing.[37]

---

[33] 43 CFR 3102.2-1–3103.3-4.

[34] 43 CFR 3103.3-6–3103.3-7.

[35] 43 CFR 3105.1-1–3105.5-2.

[36] 43 CFR 3110.1-1.

[37] 43 CFR 3110.1-2–3110.1-6.

In the case of simultaneous offers, the procedure is as follows. On the third Monday of each month each office must post a list of lands having leases which expired, were canceled, were relinquished, or which terminated, together with a notice that such lands will be subject to simultaneous filings from the time of posting until 10:00 A.M. on the fifth working day thereafter. Offers to lease such lands must be submitted on a Simultaneous Oil and Gas Entry Card that has been signed and executed by the applicant or his agent. The card must be accompanied by a remittance covering the filing fee of $10. Only one leasing unit, identified by parcel number, may be included in one entry card. Three entry cards must be drawn for each numbered leasing unit, and the order in which they are drawn fixes priorities. (If less than three cards are filed, all are drawn.) Unsuccessful drawees must be notified by the return of their cards. A lease will be issued to the first drawee qualified to receive a lease upon payment of the first year's rental. The rental must be received in the proper office of the BLM within fifteen days of notice that such payment is due.[38]

Competitive Oil and Gas Leases. The regulation states, "All competitive leases shall be for a primary term of 5 years and so long thereafter as oil or gas is produced in paying quantities."[39] The lands subject to disposition by competitive bidding (lands within known geological structures of producing fields) must be divided into tracts not exceeding 640 acres in size. Each such tract forms a leasing unit. Notice of the offer of lands for leasing, at specified royalty and rental rates, to the qualified bidder offering the highest bonus by competitive bidding either at public auction or by sealed bids, as stated in the notice, must be published once a week for five consecutive weeks in a newspaper of general circulation in the county in which the lands are located, or in such other publications that the authorized officer of the BLM may designate. The notice must state, among other things, the time and place of sale, the manner of submitting bids, description of the lands, and conditions of sale. Each successful bidder in an auction sale, and each bidder in a sealed-bid sale, must submit along with his bid a certified check, money order, or cash amounting to one-fifth of his bid. Following the auction or the opening of sealed bids, the authorized

[38] 43 CFR 3112.1-2–3112.4-1.
[39] 43 CFR 3120.1-1.

officer, subject to his right to reject any or all bids, will award the lease to the successful bidder. Three copies of the lease must be sent to the latter, who must not later than the fifteenth day following receipt, or the thirtieth day after the sale, whichever is later, execute the lease, pay the balance of his bonus bid plus the first year's rental, and file the bond mentioned above. The bidder who fails to comply with these requirements forfeits his deposit. Deposits on rejected bids must be returned to bidders.[40]

OIL SHALE

As for oil shale, the secretary of the interior is authorized by the Mineral Leasing Act to lease to any qualified person or corporation deposits of oil shale, native asphalt, solid and semisolid bitumen and bituminous rock, and the surface of so much of the public lands containing such deposits or lying adjacent thereto as may be required for extraction and reduction. No lease shall exceed 5,120 acres of land. Leases may be for indeterminate periods, subject to such conditions as the secretary may impose concerning methods of mining and prevention of waste and productive development. For the privilege of mining, extracting, and disposing of oil from the lease, the lessee shall pay a royalty at the rate specified in the lease and an annual rental, creditable against royalty, of 50 cents per acre per annum. The royalty rate is subject to readjustment by the secretary at the end of each twenty years. For the purpose of encouraging shale oil production, the secretary may waive the payment of royalty and rental during the first five years of a lease. No person, association, or corporation may hold more than one oil shale lease.[41]

THE ACQUIRED LANDS LEASING ACT OF 1947

The Acquired Lands Leasing Act of 1947 applies to lands acquired by the United States,[42] as distinguished from lands in the "original" public domain, to which the mineral-leasing laws have not been previ-

---

[40] 43 CFR 3120.1-3–3120.4-2.
[41] 30 U.S.C. 241.
[42] 30 U.S.C. 351–359.

ously extended. It provides generally for the leasing of all deposits of coal, phosphate, oil, oil shale, gas, sodium, potassium, and sulfur within such lands (other than lands situated in cities, towns, villages, national parks or monuments, military reservations, tidelands, or submerged lands) under the same conditions as provided in the mineral leasing laws (chiefly, the Mineral Leasing Act of 1920).[43]

THE OUTER CONTINENTAL SHELF LANDS ACT OF 1953

The Outer Continental Shelf Lands Act of 1953[44] provides for U.S. jurisdiction over the submerged lands of the outer continental shelf (seaward of state boundaries) and authorizes the secretary of the interior to lease such lands for minerals production.[45] It provides that the secretary shall administer the provisions of the act relating to the leasing of outer continental shelf lands, and shall prescribe rules and regulations necessary to that end. The secretary is authorized to prescribe and amend such rules and regulations as he determines to be necessary and proper in order to prevent the waste of the natural resources of the outer continental shelf, and to protect correlative rights therein. He is authorized to cooperate with the conservation agencies of adjacent states in the enforcement of conservation laws, rules, and regulations. The rules and regulations prescribed by the secretary "may provide for the assignment or relinquishment of leases, for the sale of royalty oil and gas accruing or reserved to the United States at not less than market value, and, in the interest of conservation, for unitization, pooling, drilling agreements, suspension of operations or production, reduction of rentals or royalties, compensatory royalty agreements, subsurface storage of oil or gas in any of said submerged lands, and drilling or other easements necessary for operations or production."[46]

Any person who knowingly and willfully violates any rule or regulation prescribed by the secretary for the prevention of waste, the conservation of natural resources, or the protection of correlative rights is subject to a fine of not more than $2,000, or to imprisonment for not

[43] 30 U.S.C. 351–352.
[44] 43 U.S.C. 1331–1343.
[45] 43 U.S.C. 1332–1333.
[46] 43 U.S.C. 1334(a)(1).

more than six months.[47] Whenever the owner of a *nonproducing* lease fails to comply with any of the provisions of the act, or of a lease or regulations issued under the act, the lease may be canceled by the secretary, subject to the right of judicial review.[48] Whenever the owner of a *producing* lease fails to comply with any provision of the act, or of a lease or regulations issued under the act, such a lease may be forfeited and canceled by an appropriate proceeding in a U.S. district court having jurisdiction.[49]

> The Secretary is authorized to grant to the highest responsible qualified bidder by competitive bidding under regulations promulgated in advance, oil and gas leases on submerged lands of the Outer Continental Shelf. . . . The bidding shall be (1) by sealed bids, and (2) at the discretion of the Secretary, on the basis of a cash bonus with a royalty fixed by the Secretary at not less than 12½ per centum in amount or value of the production saved, removed or sold, or on the basis of royalty, but at not less than the per centum above mentioned, with a cash bonus fixed by the Secretary.[50]
>
> An oil and gas lease . . . shall (1) cover a compact area not exceeding five thousand seven hundred and sixty acres, as the Secretary may determine, (2) be for a period of five years and as long thereafter as oil or gas may be produced from the area in paying quantities, or drilling or well reworking operations as approved by the Secretary are conducted thereon, (3) require the payment of a royalty of not less than 12½ per centum, . . . and (4) contain such rental provisions and such other terms and provisions as the Secretary may prescribe at the time of offering the area for lease.[51]

Notice of sale of leases, and the terms of bidding, must be published at least thirty days before the date of sale. The secretary may cancel any lease obtained by fraud or misrepresentation. Proceeds from lease sales, including rents and royalties, shall be deposited with the Treasury of the United States and credited to miscellaneous receipts.[52]

The regulation reads, "Any agency of the United States and any person authorized by the Secretary may conduct geological and geo-

[47] 43 U.S.C. 1334(a)(2).
[48] 43 U.S.C. 1334(b)(1).
[49] 43 U.S.C. 1334(b)(2).
[50] 43 U.S.C. 1337(a).
[51] 43 U.S.C. 1337(b).
[52] 43 U.S.C. 1337(f)–(1) and 1338.

physical explorations in the Outer Continental Shelf, which do not interfere with or endanger actual operations under any lease maintained or granted pursuant to this Act, and which are not unduly harmful to aquatic life in such area."[53]

Some Amplifying Outer Continental Shelf Regulations

The BLM is required to prepare, as needed, official leasing maps of areas of the outer continental shelf, made to conform so far as practicable to the method of tract designation established by the adjoining state. The boundaries of mineral leases are to be described in accordance with such maps. Any area so mapped is subject to lease if not withdrawn or restricted from operation under the enabling act.[54]

From time to time the director may announce tentative schedules of lease sales. As each area is initially considered for mineral leasing, or as the need arises, the director shall request the Geological Survey to prepare a report describing the general geology and potential mineral resources of the area. In addition, the director shall request that other interested federal agencies prepare reports describing what other valuable resources are contained within the area and the potential effect of mineral operations upon such resources or upon the total environment.[55]

In selecting tracts for mineral leasing, the director must receive and consider nominations of tracts by potential lessees, or, from time to time upon approval of the secretary, may issue calls for nominations.[56] Prior to the final selection of tracts for leasing, the director

Shall evaluate fully the potential effect of the leasing program on the total environment, aquatic resources, aesthetics, recreation, and other resources in the entire area during exploration, development and operational phases. To aid him in his evaluation and determinations he shall request and consider the views and recommendations of appropriate Federal agencies, may hold public hearings after appropriate notice, and may consult with State agencies, organizations, industries, and individ-

[53] 43 U.S.C. 1340.
[54] 43 U.S.C. 3301.1.
[55] 43 CFR 3301.2.
[56] 43 CFR 3301.3.

uals. The Director shall develop special leasing stipulations and conditions when necessary to protect the environment and all other resources, and such special stipulations and conditions shall be contained in the proposed notice of lease offer. The proposed notice of lease offer, together with all views and recommendations received and the Director's findings or actions thereon, shall be submitted to the Secretary for final approval.[57]

Upon approval of the secretary, the director shall publish the notice of lease offer, at least thirty days in advance, in the *Federal Register,* and in such other publications as may be desirable. The notice must state the place and time of filing bids, the place and time of opening bids, and any special stipulations or conditions, including those for environmental protection, which will become a part of the lease granted pursuant to the notice.[58]

The regulation states, "Upon direction of the Secretary, the Director, after obtaining the recommendation of the Director, Geological Survey, is authorized to publish on his own motion notices of lease offer of tracts which have been determined by the Director, Geological Survey, to be subject to drainage of their oil and gas deposits from wells on other tracts."[59] The director may request the views and recommendations of appropriate federal and state agencies prior to offering drainage lease sales.

A separate bid must be submitted for each lease unit, and for not less than the entire unit. Each bid must be accompanied by a certified check or its equivalent for one-fifth of the amount of the bonus offered, evidence of citizenship if appropriate, articles of association or incorporation as appropriate, and evidence of authority of the person bidding. The regulation reads, "All bidders are warned against violation of the provisions of Title 18 U.S.C. section 1860, prohibiting unlawful combination or intimidation of bidders."[60]

Sealed bids received on leases offered shall be opened at the time and place indicated in the notice. Bids are publicly announced and recorded, but none is accepted or rejected at that time. Although leases may be awarded only to the highest qualified and responsible bidder, the United States reserves the discretionary right to reject any and all

[57] 43 CFR 3301.4.
[58] 43 CFR 3301.5.
[59] 43 CFR 3301.6.
[60] 43 CFR 3302.4.

bids received for a tract, regardless of amount. Awards are made only by written notice accompanied by lease forms for execution. Tie bids are rejected unless within fifteen days after notification the bidders involved file with the director an agreement to accept the lease jointly. If the authorized officer of the United States fails to accept the highest bid within thirty days of opening, all bids on the affected lease are considered rejected. In any case, notice of action must be promptly transmitted to the several bidders. If the lease is awarded, the successful bidder is sent three copies and is required to execute them, to pay the first year's rental and the balance of the bonus bid, and to file a bond within fifteen days of receipt or thirty days following the lease sale, whichever is later. Deposits on rejected bids are returned. If the successful bidder fails to execute the lease or otherwise comply with regulations, his deposit is forfeited.[61]

An annual rental, at the rate specified in the lease, shall be due and payable on the first day of each lease year prior to a discovery. Royalties shall be paid at the rate specified in the lease, but in no event shall the royalty on oil and gas be less than 12½ percent of the amount or value of the production saved, removed or sold from the lease. Each lessee shall pay the minimum royalty specified in the lease at the end of each lease year beginning with the first lease year following a discovery on the lease.[62] In the event that the oil and gas supervisor of the Geological Survey directs the suspension of operations and production on a lease, or operations where there is no production, no payment of rental or minimum royalty shall be required during the period of suspension.[63]

THE MINING AND MINERALS POLICY ACT OF 1970

The Mining and Minerals Policy Act of 1970[64] declares that the continuing policy of the federal government is to foster and encourage private enterprise in, among other things, "the orderly and economic development of domestic mineral resources."[65]

---

[61] 43 CFR 3302.5.
[62] 43 CFR 3303.1–3303.3.
[63] 43 CFR 3303.5(a).
[64] 30 U.S.C. 21a.
[65] Ibid.

THE NATIONAL ENVIRONMENTAL POLICY ACT OF 1969

The National Environmental Policy Act of 1969[66] declares it to be the "continuing policy of the Federal Government, in cooperation with state and local governments, and other concerned public and private organizations, to use all practicable means and measures . . . to create and maintain conditions under which man and nature can exist in productive harmony."[67] It further declares it to be the "continuing responsibility of the Federal Government to use all practicable means . . . to improve and coordinate federal plans, functions, programs, and resources to the end that the Nation may (1) fulfill the responsibilities of each generation as trustee of the environment for succeeding generations; (2) assume for all Americans safe, healthful, productive, and esthetically and culturally pleasing surroundings; (3) attain the widest range of beneficial uses of the environment without degradation, risk to health or safety, or other undesirable and unintended consequences."[68]

The act directs that all agencies of the federal government shall, among other things, "include in every recommendation or report on proposals for legislation and other major Federal actions significantly affecting the quality of the human environment, a detailed statement by the responsible official on (i) the environmental impact of the proposed action."[69] Prior to making the statement, the responsible official shall consult with other relevant federal agencies. Copies of the statement and the comments and views of appropriate federal, state, and local agencies shall be made available to the president, the Council on Environmental Quality (created elsewhere in the act), and the public.[70]

TITLE 31 U.S.C. 483

This section of Title 31 declares it to be the sense of Congress that any permit (among other things) granted by a federal agency shall be

[66] 42 U.S.C. 4321–4347.
[67] 42 U.S.C. 4331(a).
[68] 42 U.S.C. 4331(b).
[69] 42 U.S.C. 4332.
[70] Ibid.

self-sustaining to the fullest extent possible, and it authorizes the heads of federal agencies to prescribe fees, charges, or prices that are fair and equitable.[71]

A SUMMARY OF LEASING PRACTICE

The manner of leasing onshore lands for oil and gas production depends upon whether the lands in question have been determined to be within the known geological structure of an oil and gas field. If so determined, the lands must be leased by competitive bidding, either by auction or by sealed bids, after public advertisement, in units not exceeding 640 acres, for a primary term of five years and so long thereafter as oil or gas is produced in paying quantities. The royalty rate is specified in the lease, but it may not be less than 12½ percent. Subject to the right of refusal, each lease is granted to the qualified bidder offering the highest lease bonus. Lands not determined to be within a known geological structure, and so forth, are leased non-competitively, in units not exceeding 2,560 acres, for a primary term of two years and so long thereafter as oil or gas is produced in paying quantities, to the first qualified bidder at a royalty of 12½ percent. In the case of lands covered by expired, canceled, relinquished, or termi-nated prior leases, availability is advertised monthly. If more than one offer to lease is received within five days, priorities are determined by a public drawing. A filing fee of $10 per offer, but no bonus, is re-quired.

Oil and gas leases on the outer continental shelf must be granted competitively. From time to time the responsible officer of the BLM, having considered the nominations of potential lessees, selects tracts for leasing in units not to exceed 5,760 acres in size. After advertisement at least thirty days in advance, the officer opens publicly all sealed bids on each unit and, subject to the right of refusal, awards a lease to the qualified bidder offering the largest lease bonus. (The law authorizes royalty bidding, but only a few such sales, of an experimental nature, have been conducted.) Leases are for a primary term of five years and can be continued only so long thereafter as oil or gas is produced in

[71] 31 U.S.C. 483a.

paying quantities. The royalty rate is specified in the lease; it is ordinarily 16⅔ percent, but may not be less than 12½ percent.

Since the passage of the Federal Coal Leasing Amendments Act of 1975 (Public Law 94-377, August 4, 1976), coal leases on onshore federal lands may be awarded only on the basis of competitive (bonus) bidding, with a royalty rate prescribed at not less than 12½ percent. Tract size is determined at the discretion of the secretary of the interior. Leases are granted for a term of twenty years and so long thereafter as coal is produced in commercial quantities. Leases are subject to a comprehensive land use plan embracing the affected coal resources. Exploration licenses may be issued, but such licenses confer no right to a lease.

There are no general regulations other than statutory provisions applying to oil-shale leasing, but in the only sale of such leases, which took place in 1974, each lease was awarded to the applicant bidding the largest lease bonus for a term of twenty years and so long thereafter as production continues in commercial quantities. The basic royalty rate specified was 12 cents per ton of shale processed, this rate being adjusted up or down as the yield of oil rises above or falls below 30 gallons per ton. Terms and conditions were made readjustable at the end of twenty years. No lease exceeded 5,120 acres in size, and each applicant was restricted to one lease.

3

The Relevant Economics—
Economic Rent

In this chapter and in chapter 4 we will develop an economic framework of analysis. This framework is applicable to all the minerals under discussion and is fundamental to our treatment of specific issues in later chapters. Its full development here, rather than piecemeal in connection with separate issues, not only establishes at the outset the nature of our approach and criteria of evaluation, but permits a more concise and pointed treatment of the issues when they are taken up. The framework is developed from elementary propositions in economics for the benefit of those readers who may have limited training in that discipline.

As indicated above, we shall argue that the Department of the Interior, as custodian of the affected federal lands, should lease lands for minerals production on such terms and conditions, and at such a rate, as will tend to maximize the present value of the pure economic rent derivable from them. In order to justify such a policy it is necessary to explain the nature and origin of pure economic rent, and to show that its maximization is the equivalent of maximizing the value of the lands in question to society as a whole. Such are the tasks of the present chapter.

DEFINITION OF ECONOMIC RENT

In common parlance the term *rent* means the payment a lessee makes to a lessor for the use of a physical asset—a farm, a house, a car, and so forth—for a specified period of time. Economists mean something rather different by rent, and in order to distinguish their term from the layman's they commonly add the qualifier *economic. Economic rent,* in the economist's current usage, means any surplus in the income of a factor of production—land, labor, or capital—where *surplus* is the excess of the factor's income over the minimum amount necessary to call forth its productive services. Thus a worker who would be willing to perform his labor services for $3 per hour but is in fact paid $4 per hour receives an economic rent of the difference, that is, $1 per hour.

Clearly, such a surplus could arise only where the supply of the factor of production is less than perfectly elastic; for if the supply were perfectly elastic, the quantity supplied would expand in response to the least surplus and immediately wipe it out. Rents that arise out of purely short-term inelasticities of supply are called *quasi rents,* because they tend to disappear in the long run, that is, a period of time long enough for the quantity of the factor supplied to respond fully to the inducement of its income. True rents, then, are due to inelasticity of the long-run supplies of productive factors.

The classic case of long-run inelasticity of supply is that of land, where the term *land* embraces all raw natural resources. Indeed, it was because land is a distinguishable factor of production and the payment for its use is called rent that the classic economists conceived of rent as a form of income distinct from wages, interest, and profits; and it is because the rent of land is in the character of a surplus that the concept of rent has gradually evolved to embrace all surpluses. Land viewed as all raw natural resources is by definition a gift of nature. It is not and cannot be produced by man, and therefore its supply is completely inelastic with respect to its income, even in the long run. Its income is entirely economic rent.

It is true, of course, that land may have more than one use and that its supply for a specific use may be quite elastic. Thus if certain land may be used for strip-mining of coal or for grazing, but not for both, the supply of land for strip-mining becomes perfectly elastic where the rent from strip-mining coincides with the rent from grazing. Landlords seek to maximize their rental incomes, so they grant leases to those offering the highest rent. If the rent offered by strip miners falls below that offered by cattle- or sheepmen, then the land in question will be denied to strip miners. But the fact that rent is paid at all is due to the inelastic supply of land for all uses taken together.

In saying that all the income of land is economic rent we are, of course, strictly defining land as raw natural resources, entirely a gift of nature. Improvements on land—roads, ditches, terraces, and the like —being man-made, have some elasticity of supply with respect to the incomes they command. And a landlord owning improved land tends to receive a contractual rent which is in part return on his investment in improvements. Moreover, a landlord who has purchased raw land may rightly view his rental income as simply a return on investment. The fact remains, however, that his investment is the capitalized value of expected economic rent and does not alter the supply or earning capacity of land. No real capital is formed, and the landlord's income is not return to capital in a social sense. On the other hand, such a landlord need receive no "surplus." In this case, if the buyer and his competitors have correctly anticipated the land's rental income, the surplus tends to accrue to the seller—perhaps to all past sellers taken together—but the income yielded to the buyer is economic rent and the real source of the surplus.

We have asserted that the Department of the Interior should attempt to maximize the present value of pure economic rent. By *pure economic rent* we mean the income which arises strictly from the scarcity value of land as defined, unalloyed by any other element of income. For example, as suggested above, pure economic rent excludes the return on investment in improvements. It also excludes positive or negative elements in contractual rents that reflect monopolistic restraints of supply on the side of either lessors or lessees, or that reflect externalities in land use. Finally, it ideally excludes positive or negative elements in contractual rents that reflect lack of knowledge by lessors or lessees.

Full knowledge and the absence of any element of monopoly are implied by the condition of perfect competition. Accordingly, for the purposes of this study—which is concerned solely with the leasing of land and hence with land rent—we define pure economic rent as the income which tends to accrue in the long run, under conditions of perfect competition and the absence of externalities, to the owners of land, where "land" is raw natural resources. While no one supposes that perfect competition ever did or could exist, land rents that would arise under that condition are an objective that the Department of the Interior may more closely approach with suitably designed terms and conditions of land leasing. The task of showing how this can come about begins with the above definition.

THE THEORY OF ECONOMIC RENT

The income of a factor of production—land, labor, or capital—per unit engaged is a price determined by the supply of and demand for that factor. The supply of a factor is a schedule of the number of units of it that are offered for hire at different factor prices. Generally, except in the case of land as we have defined it, the quantities offered for hire increase with factor prices, other prices, or the general price level given. This fact reflects increasing disutility at the margin associated with increasing quantity of the factor supplied. The demand for a factor is a schedule of the number of units of it that users are willing to hire at different factor prices, with the quantities demanded varying inversely with factor prices. The inverse relationship reflects declining marginal productivity of the factor as increasing amounts of it are employed relative to other factors. Indeed, under conditions of perfect competition, the schedule of marginal productivity of a factor multiplied by the price of output *is* the demand schedule for the factor; for by pushing employment to the point where factor price equals the value of the marginal product, competitive employers tend to maximize profits.

Consider now the market for land. As we stated earlier, land, as defined, is not producible by man; no cost is incurred in its creation. It will not go away if its owner receives no income from it, and no owner can make himself better off by withholding land from productive combination with labor and capital. Its supply, therefore, is perfectly inelastic with respect to its income. Figure 3-1 illustrates the determination of land's income, all rent, assuming for the time being that land is homogeneous.

Here SS is the supply curve of land, perfectly vertical at OL_e, which measures the total quantity of land in acres. DD is the demand for land, corresponding to the value of the marginal product of land (VMP). R_e is the equilibrium price (income per unit). The area OR_eEL_e is economic rent and the total income of land. Thus all the income of land is the surplus that we call economic rent. It is in no sense compensation for a social cost. It becomes a private cost to the users of land because competition among users will assure that all units of a homogeneous supply receive the same price, and that the price will correspond to the value of the marginal product where all land is employed.

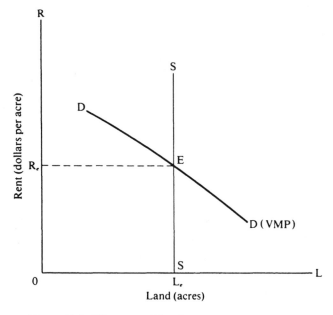

Figure 3-1. The rent of land.

It should be apparent from figure 3-1 that the rent per unit of land will rise (or fall) if the schedule of *VMP* (*DD*) rises (or falls). *VMP* may rise either because the price of the product of land rises or because the schedule of marginal productivity rises. The latter may occur because of a technological improvement or in consequence of an increase in the input of labor or capital. Pure economic rent tends to be maximized when the most productive technology is employed and the inputs of land and capital correspond to the equilibrium quantities determined by their respective supplies and demands. Since the marginal productivity of any factor depends in part on the inputs of other factors, there must be a simultaneous determination of equilibrium inputs and prices in all factor markets. In our further discussion of the rent of land we shall assume the appropriate equilibrium values in labor and capital markets.

Land has many possible uses, of course; and there is a different *VMP* schedule corresponding to each use. Thus, in figure 3-2, the use of given units of land for strip mining might present the schedule VMP_m, for agriculture VMP_a, and for building space VMP_s, these three uses are assumed to be mutually exclusive. R_m is the equilibrium rent per unit

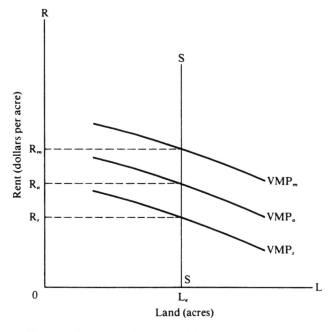

Figure 3-2. Competing uses of land.

from mining, R_a from agriculture, and R_s from building space. If the land in question were homogeneous, it would be used only for mining, for miners would be able to compete the land away from other uses. The owners of land would naturally lease the land to the users offering the highest rent. Thus the competitive determination of rent is associated with the allocation of available land to its most productive use.

If two or more uses of land are not entirely mutually exclusive— such as underground mining and timber production, or agriculture and oil production (through widely spaced wells)—then land will tend to be allocated to the *combination* of uses yielding the highest rent. The combination need not be simultaneous but may be sequential. Thus a sequence of strip-mining, surface restoration, and grazing may yield a higher rent, reduced to present value, than would continuous grazing.

Land is not homogeneous, of course. Different parcels of land have different productive attributes. Consequently, the highest rent will be yielded by mining on some land, grazing on other land, agriculture on still other land, and so forth, and there will be a corresponding allocation of land among different uses. Among parcels of land devoted

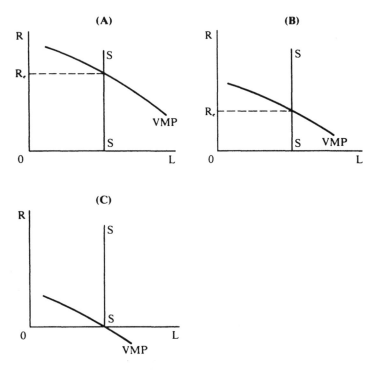

Figure 3-3. Land quality and rent.

to the same use, schedules of marginal productivity differ, so that different parcels yield different levels of rent. Thus, other things being constant, land containing mineral deposits that are relatively deep, or otherwise relatively inaccessible, will yield less rent per unit than more favored land.

This last point may be illustrated by means of figure 3-3A–C. In each panel the quantity of land with given productive attributes (for a use such as minerals production) is represented by a vertical supply curve. The quality of land decreases from figure 3-3A to figure 3-3C, as indicated by lower and lower schedules of VMP. Rent per unit declines accordingly from 3-3A land to 3-3C land. The land represented in figure 3-3C is just marginal, barely yielding enough to cover costs (including a normal competitive return on capital) and generating no rent. To the right of figure 3-3C, we can conceptualize additional diagrams, representing increasingly submarginal lands not presently in use for the purpose in question.

Now suppose there is either a rise in the price of the product of the above land or an improvement in production technology. All the VMP schedules will shift upward; rents will rise on all land; land, as shown in figure 3-3C, will become supramarginal and yield rent; and land, as shown in figure 3-3D, will become marginal. Thus, as technological progress occurs or demand for a product of land grows, or both, additional land tends to come into use for the production of that product in the order of the productivity of the land. The competitive determination of rent is associated, then, with a tendency to use the best land first, which implies that at any given time production occurs from that collection of land that is most productive. Also, the existence at any time of large amounts of submarginal land implies the capacity to expand production of a product of land in response to either a cost reduction or a demand-induced rise in price. Products of land, such as minerals, do not abruptly run out; the margin of land use in their production simply expands until they yield their place in competitive markets to substitute products.

It is important to note that land may be marginal or submarginal for a given use, and thus would yield no rent in that use, but supramarginal for some alternative use. The alternative use would prevail, then, yielding rent to the landowner, until costs fell or prices rose sufficiently in the given use to generate a still higher rent, thus permitting competitive displacement of the alternative use.

In most uses of land, such as agriculture, grazing, timber growing, and the provision of building sites, the capacity of the land to yield rent is not necessarily reduced by the production of land services. The case is different with the production of minerals. As minerals are extracted from given parcels of land, the real cost of extracting still more tends to rise (the VMP schedule tends to shift down) until eventually the land becomes submarginal, and extraction from it ceases. The principle may be illustrated by means of figure 3-3A–C. Let it represent the status of a given parcel of land at different points in time, with the degree of exhaustion increasing from figure 3-3A to figure 3-3C. Early in the life of minerals extraction the rent yielded is high; but rent declines with exhaustion and eventually falls to zero, at which time the extraction of minerals ceases. (Indeed, minerals extraction will cease when the rent it yields falls below that yielded by some other use if leases may be recontracted at frequent intervals.)

Thus land rent from minerals extraction is a temporary source of income, one that seldom ends abruptly but usually dwindles gradually to nothing. Among the implications this may have, we may note that, first, the time pattern of rent from minerals extraction is relevant to its evaluation. It may be possible to compare two alternative streams of rent only by reducing them through the discounting process to present value. Second, the use of land for minerals extraction must yield at some future time to some other use. It is therefore relevant to the evaluation of rent from minerals extraction that such extraction may affect the productivity of land in some alternative use. For example, strip-mining of coal in certain situations may not allow return of overburden and restoration of grass cover, so that the land in question is lost forever to grazing. Again, the evaluation and comparison of alternative rents may necessitate discounting to present value.

AN ALTERNATIVE APPROACH

For some purposes it will be useful to us to approach the theory of rent in another way, through the theory of the firm or plant. Again, we will assume, for the time being, perfect competition, and we will consider the firm or plant in its long-run adjustment to price and cost stimuli. (The "long run" is a period of time long enough to allow full adjustment to stimuli, including a change in capacity.) Imagine a group of identical plants using identical land in identical proportions with labor and capital, one of which is represented in figure 3-4A. Assume the initial price per unit of output is P_o, which is equal to the long-run average cost (LAC) at its lowest point, and, therefore, equal to long-run marginal cost (LMC). Equilibrium output is Q_{ae}, at which point the plant is earning the normal competitive return on the investment embodied in LAC. It cannot expand or contract output without reducing the rate of return, since LAC would then exceed price. Price being equal to LAC, which includes no land rent, the operation pays no rent to the owners of the land used. (This implies, of course, that the land has no rent-yielding alternative.) The plant, represented in figure 3-3B, located on inferior land, is a hypothetical one. It cannot exist in long-run equilibrium because its LAC is everywhere in excess of P_o.

Now suppose that because of an increased demand for the product in question, say, a mineral, the price per unit rises to P_1. Immediately, a

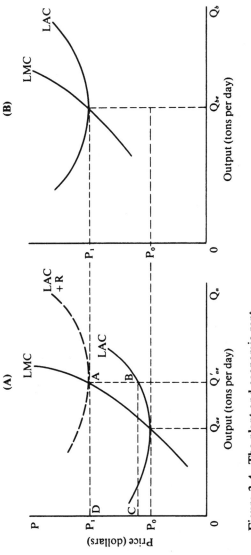

Figure 3-4. The plant and economic rent.

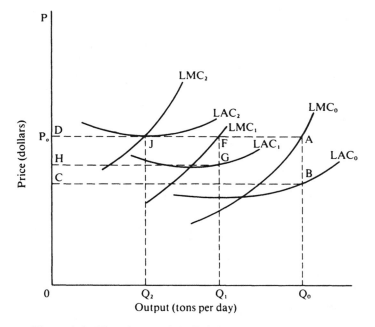

Figure 3-5. The plant and declining rent.

plant in the situation shown in figure 3-4A begins to make above-normal profits. Existing firms and outsiders now compete for the quality land, offering rent to landowners and bidding up the rent per unit of output until the total unit cost, LAC plus rent (R) per unit is once again equal to price, and rates of return are normal. In the new equilibrium the plant in the situation shown in figure 3-4A is producing Q'_{ae}, where $LAC + R = LMC =$ price P_1. The plant is paying rent per unit of output AB and total rent $ABCD$, which is $AB \times OQ'_{ae}$. Note that rent is paid because the price has risen; the price did not rise because rent is paid.

Simultaneously with the adjustments on lands represented in figure 3-4A, new plants are being constructed on lands represented by figure 3-4B. On these lands the typical plant will produce Q_{be}, corresponding to the lowest point on its LAC; it will earn a normal competitive return on investment, and will pay no rent since $LAC = LMC = P_1$.

If the price should rise above P_1, additional lands would be brought into use, the lands shown in figure 3-4B would yield rent, and the lands

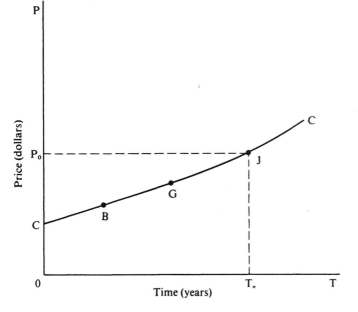

Figure 3-6. Falling rent with depletion.

shown in figure 3-4*A* would yield still larger rents, and so forth. The rent rises because the price rises, not vice versa.

A diagram similar to that shown in figure 3-4*A* can be used to illustrate the dwindling of rent on a given parcel of land as the minerals on it become progressively depleted. In figure 3-5, the initial situation is given by LAC_o, LMC_o, and P_o, so that output is Q_o and rent paid is *ABCD*. As minerals from the parcel of land are depleted, the plant's costs rise to LAC_1 and LMC_1, output falls to Q_1, and rent declines to *FGHD*. When costs rise to LAC_2 and LMC_2, rent disappears and shortly thereafter production on the given parcel of land ceases.

It is also possible to depict the rise in costs on a given parcel of land as minerals are depleted over time, as is shown in figure 3-6. Points on the cost curve *CC*, moving from left to right, correspond to points such as *B*, *G*, and *J* in figure 3-5. Time (T) is on the horizontal axis of figure 3-6, and T_n corresponds to the point in time when production ceases. The vertical distance between *CC* and P_oJ is rent paid per unit of production. Clearly, a reduction of costs on the given parcel of land would increase rent paid, given the price P_o, and extend the economic life of the mineral deposit.[1]

THE CONTRACTUAL FORM OF RENT PAYMENT

Up to this point we have implicitly assumed that land rent is paid in cash as it is earned. Under conditions of perfect competition, which assumes perfect knowledge, this is a reasonable assumption, although an equally reasonable assumption would be that the present value of expected rent is paid at the time a lease is contracted. In neither case is the extensive nor the intensive margin of land use affected by rent. The margin is simultaneously determined with price by demand and costs other than rent.

In the real world of imperfect knowledge, however, the rent payment may take another form, that of a share in output. In minerals production this share is ordinarily called a *royalty*, signifying originally the crown's share in the output of mines. If the royalty rate is fixed, regardless of the cost of minerals production in relation to price, then the royalty affects the margin of land use for minerals extraction and also, to a degree, the price of extracted minerals. This seems to contradict our earlier repeated assertion that rent is price determined, not price determining, but it does so only by appearance. Pure economic rent, as defined, does not affect price, but a fixed royalty as a contractual rent form generally does not coincide precisely with pure economic rent. It is the nature of the contract, not the nature of economic rent, that causes the rent payment to affect price.

Before illustrating this point, it is useful to observe that in American minerals production contractual rent payments typically take all of three different forms: a lease bonus, a delay rental, and a royalty. The lease bonus is paid as a lump sum at the time a lease is granted by the landowner. The delay rental is a periodic payment, usually nominal in size, that is made to the landowner until the lease expires or production begins, whichever occurs first. The royalty, as indicated above, is the payment to the landowner of a share in such production as occurs, or

---

[1] Note that the curve CC in figure 3-6 is not a longer-run cost curve comparable to LAC, but is merely the locus of equilibrium points on successive LAC curves as capacity declines over time.

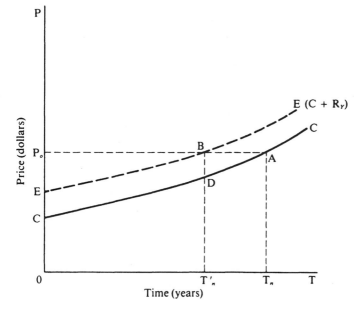

Figure 3-7. Royalty and lease bonus in rent.

its cash equivalent. In our discussion we shall concentrate on the lease bonus and the royalty.

Consider figure 3-7, which is based on figure 3-6, and represents one parcel of land on which minerals production occurs. There is a given price P_o, shown on the vertical axis. Time is on the horizontal axis. CC represents points on the extractor's long-run average cost curves as depletion occurs (see figure 3-5). The distance between CC and P_oA is the pure economic rent per unit, and T_n is the time when extraction ceases if rent is paid either as a lease bonus or as a periodic payment equal to rent currently earned. The lease bonus would be the present value at time zero of a stream of rent payments determined by multiplying the amount of unit rent in each time period by the output of the period. Given the time pattern of output, the lease bonus is proportionate to the area of P_oAC.

Suppose, however, a royalty per unit of CE is paid in addition to a lease bonus. The cost curve relevant to the abandonment decision becomes EE (CC + royalty) and the abandonment time T'_n. The lease bonus at time zero would now be proportionate to P_oBE. The total rent in present value at time zero would be proportionate to P_oBDC, which is smaller than P_oAC by BAD. Thus, total mineral production from the parcel of land and the present value at time zero of the rental income are both reduced by the contractual provision for a royalty.[2]

It must be emphasized that, in figure 3-7, pure economic rent per unit remains the difference between P_oA and CC, and that such rent does not affect the margin of exploitation or price. It is the fixity of the royalty beyond T_n' which contracts the margin and raises price. To illustrate, suppose that beginning at time T_n' the royalty becomes flexible and declines, as the distance between P_oA and CC declines, reaching zero at time T_n. Now the total rent paid—the lease bonus plus royalty—coincides with pure economic rent, while the margin of exploitation and price are unaffected.

UNCERTAINTY AND ECONOMIC RENT

The question naturally arises, Why is a royalty paid? Why does land rent not take the form exclusively of a lease bonus or an annual rental payment? Although there is undoubtedly much that is simply conventional in the persistence of royalty arrangements, we suggest that the principal answer to the above questions is that at the time a mineral lease contract is made there is uncertainty on the side of both parties to the contract as to the quantity of minerals available, the costs of their extraction, the price at which they can be sold, and, hence, the amount of pure economic rent that will be generated. "Uncertainty" in an undertaking, as distinguished from "risk," means that the probability distribution of possible outcomes is not exactly known. If the land-

---

[2] It is implicitly assumed here that installed capacity would not be affected by the introduction of a royalty. In reality, it is likely that the introduction of a royalty would induce operators to install less capacity. (With a royalty to pay, less transfer of cash flow from future to present can be accomplished by a given increment to capacity; hence the less profitable an increment would be.) Thus, relative to a pure lease bonus situation, the time to abandonment need not be shortened. However, the present value of rent receipts would be reduced and, depending upon the effect of capacity on marginal extraction costs, ultimate recovery might also be reduced.

owner were certain about the amount of pure economic rent available, he would never consent to a provision in the lease that would reduce his income below that figure, as we have just seen that a royalty provision would do. If competitive miners were certain, they would bid against each other for a lease until all the pure economic rent was promised to the landowner; and if their creditors were certain, the miners would be able to borrow the present value of the rent and pay it all as lease bonus. But if there is uncertainty, both parties seek to hedge; a royalty arrangement tends to protect the landowner from underestimation of the rent available, and the lessee from overestimation. Individual lessor-lessee pairs are free, of course, to agree upon any combination of bonus and royalty that fits their mutual aversion to uncertainty.

Since uncertainty is nearly always present in the leasing of lands for minerals production, and since investors usually have an aversion to uncertainty, lessors would typically receive less contractual rent than the pure economic rent ultimately generated, even if the rent took the form of lease bonus or annual cash payments; and they might receive less than they would under a royalty arrangement, even though a (fixed) royalty tends to induce early abandonment, as explained above. This is because under uncertainty investors tend to estimate the future conservatively or to discount estimated values at high rates. The effect is illustrated in figure 3-8. As has been shown in figure 3-7, CC is the locus of points on a plant's long-run average cost curves, as minerals are depleted on a particular parcel of land. If there were perfect certainty, the present value of economic rent at time zero would be proportionate to the area of P_oEF. With uncertainty and a no-royalty arrangement, however, the perceived cost curve might be $C'C'$, because either costs are viewed conservatively or there is a higher rate of return on investment embodied in the long-run average cost. The present value of rent at time zero is thus reduced to a figure proportionate to P_oAH. But suppose there is provision for a royalty per unit of BD, this hedge against uncertainty making the perceived cost curve $C''C''$. The present value of rent perceived at time zero now becomes a figure proportionate to P_oBDG, of which $BDGJ$ represents the royalty component. The rent paid to the landowner is larger in the royalty case and more nearly approximates the pure economic rent generated. In effect, by providing a hedge against uncertainty, the royalty causes less pure economic rent

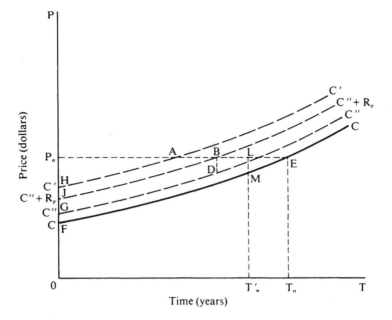

Figure 3-8. Uncertainty and rent.

to be absorbed into the lessee's rate of return as an uncertainty premium.[3]

There is another dimension of the matter, hinted at above. Where there is uncertainty, there tends to be nonprice capital rationing in financial markets. Investors are unable to borrow as much on given prospects as if costs and revenues were foreseeable with certainty. Thus investor-lessees might be unable to finance the lease bonuses they would be willing to pay if funds were available. So, for another reason, a royalty arrangement may be more consistent with maximizing pure economic rent than a straight lease-bonus arrangement.

In any case, under uncertainty the effort to maximize pure economic rent may involve a tradeoff: the higher the component of royalty in contractual rent the earlier is the abandonment point, but the lower

---

[3] Note that in both cases as production proceeds uncertainty gradually disappears, so that the cost curve CC becomes the one relevant to the abandonment decision. Thus, in the pure lease bonus case, abandonment occurs at T_n; while with a royalty of BD $(= LM)$, abandonment occurs at T_n'. The caveat in fn. 1, concerning installed capacity, applies here also.

is the rate of discount employed in evaluating income and the easier is the financing of total rental payments. This consideration suggests that there might be an optimal combination of lease bonus and royalty in each situation.

MONOPOLY AND ECONOMIC RENT

We have defined pure economic rent as that which would tend to arise under conditions of perfect competition. We have considered briefly the significance of imperfect knowledge, which lessens the perfection of competition. We must now consider the significance of elements of monopoly in the markets in which rent is determined.

If there is perfect knowledge, and there are many possible lessees for a given parcel of land, each acting independently, competition for rights to use the parcel will tend to assure that the rent contracted for will approximate the maximum amount that is consistent with a normal competitive rate of return on the part of the successful lessee. With imperfect knowledge, the rent contracted for on a given parcel of land may be higher or lower than that just indicated, but on the typical parcel it will tend to be the same (with due allowance for an uncertainty premium in lessees' rate of return). Those who typically overbid will soon fail; those who typically underbid will grow less rapidly than their competitors because they will secure fewer leases. The result need not be greatly different if there are fewer prospective lessees; but with each reduction in number the feasibility of collusion increases, as does the ability of a lessee to affect the price of his product by means of his output decisions.

Suppose that the number of prospective lessees is so small that each must take into account the change in product price that will result from a change in his own rate of output. Even if each prospective lessee acts independently of the others, the resulting rent of land for the purpose in question will be lower than if there were many competitors for access to the land. The reason is that each prospective lessee's demand will not be the value of the marginal product of land (marginal product times price), but the marginal revenue product (marginal product times marginal revenue), where marginal revenue is less than price because each increment to output is perceived as lowering the price on all units of output. The effect is illustrated in figure 3-9. There is a fixed

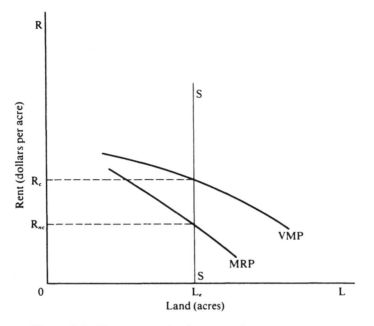

Figure 3-9. Few prospective lessees and rent.

quantity of land of homogeneous quality, indicated by the vertical supply curve *SS*. The demand for the land that would exist if there were many competitive prospective lessees is the value of the marginal product of the land (*VMP*), and the resulting rent per unit is R_c. The demand that exists with a few prospective lessees is the marginal revenue product of the land (*MRP*), and the resulting rent per unit is R_{nc}, a lower figure. In effect, some pure economic rent is transferred, in the latter case, to lessees, where it is absorbed as higher costs or a higher rate of return on investment.

It is possible, of course, that the land has more than one use and that there are many prospective lessees in the next-best use. If so, the rent of the land cannot fall below the level competitively determined for the next-best use. If in the given use the *MRP* intersects *SS* at a lower level, then the next-best use will prevail. Society will suffer as a result because its land will not be used for the socially most productive purpose.

If there is collusion among a few prospective lessees, the result will be the same as if there were one monopoly lessee. A monopolist would offer no more than the value of his *MRP* at *SS*, which would be even lower than that indicated in figure 3-9, and he would offer still less as long as his offer exceeded the competitively determined rent in some alternative use. If the monopoly *MRP* at *SS* fell below a competitive rent for an alternative use, then the collusive arrangement would break up; and only if noncollusive prospective lessees would offer lower rent than the yield of an alternative use would the alternative use prevail.

It is conceivable that monopoly elements in the market for land could exist on the side of lessors, also. Thus it will occur to the reader that the federal government, as owner or controller of vast lands suitable for minerals production, could perhaps increase the present value of its land revenues by restricting the supply available for leasing. Even if it could, which is doubtful for reasons to be detailed later, it should not. Society's welfare is maximized when all available land is supplied for use so long as the *VMP* for some use is greater than zero. Government should seek to maximize the present value of pure economic rent from its lands, not its potential revenues from such lands. Maximizing revenues may, as in this case, be inconsistent with maximizing welfare.

EXTERNALITIES

Our definition of pure economic rent contains the qualifying phrase, "and the absence of externalities." Externalities are costs or benefits borne or enjoyed by persons external to the firm or other entity causing them. For example, the oil producer who dumps waste brines into freshwater streams imposes costs on downstream users of the water, such as a community which must desalinate the water in order to render it suitable for drinking. The costs are internal to society but external to the oil producer. For an opposite example, the oil operator who engages in exploratory drilling produces information of value not only to himself but also to all other potential explorers. The benefits are internal to society but partly external to the given oil operator. These externalities could be internalized to the firms causing them by, say, imposing a tax on brine discharge into fresh water or granting a subsidy to oil exploration.

The significance of uninternalized externalities is that they result in the under- or overpricing of the products in connection with the production of which they occur, with consequent over- or underallocation of resources to the industries affected. Thus in the case of the oil producer above, the private costs, and hence price, of oil would be less than the social costs and true "price" of oil; consumers would tend to use more of it, and cause more resources to be employed in its production, than they would if they had to pay its full social cost. Over-utilization of resources in order to produce minerals results in the generation of false rents over and above the pure economic rent which the government should try to capture in the public interest. These false rents are, in effect, taxes on environmental amenities. The government as lessor should eschew them, seeking not to maximize revenues but pure economic rent. (This point will be expanded upon in the discussion of environmental protection found in chapter 4).

MAXIMIZING THE VALUE OF RESOURCES

The foregoing remarks bring us closer to the principal conclusion of this chapter, that maximizing the present value of pure economic rent is the equivalent of maximizing the value of land resources to society.

The procedure for estimating the present value of an asset is to discount the expected net proceeds, or net cash flow, from it. Suppose we have a parcel of land capable of producing minerals but nothing else, either during or after minerals extraction. Suppose that minerals extraction with the best available technique requires an initial investment (at time zero) of I_o and a stream of cash costs, beginning at time 1, of C_1, $C_2, \ldots C_n$, when n is the time of abandonment; and that there results a stream of revenues $R_1, R_2, \ldots R_n$. The value at time zero of the land, V_o, is given by the following formula, in which r is the rate of discount corresponding to the cost of capital:

$$V_o = -I_o + \frac{R_1 - C_1}{1 + r} + \frac{R_2 - C_2}{(1 + r)^2} \cdots \frac{R_n - C_n}{(1 + r)^n} \tag{3-1}$$

V_o is the maximum that a buyer in the minerals industry would be willing to pay for the land; but it is also the minimum a buyer would have to pay if he must compete for the land with numerous knowledgeable alternative buyers with equal access to the best technique of extraction. Thus, with perfect competition, the actual price of the land at time zero would tend to be V_o.

Important for our purposes, V_o is also the present value of the rent that competitive minerals extractors would offer if, as assumed, minerals extraction were the only use of the land, and if the lease acquired should run until the lessee voluntarily ceases extraction. V_o might be paid as a lease bonus or in equivalent annual installments, as the rent is generated by operations, assuming perfect competition, hence perfect knowledge. (Remember our caveat about the effect of royalty arrangements, likely to arise under uncertainty, on the present value of rent.) The price of land purchased outright is simply the present value of the rent of the land appraised by competitive potential lessees. If a lessee has full use of the land for as long as it is profitable to him, he is indifferent as between leasing and outright purchase. Conditions that would tend to maximize rent are conditions that would tend to maximize the value of the land.

V_o is the value of the land to a private user. It is also the value of the land to society, *provided* that private costs and benefits correspond to social costs and benefits. If revenues capture all benefits to society, if outlays reflect all costs to society, and if the rate of discount reflects society's rate of time preference adjusted for natural uncertainty, then the private value of the land is the same as its social value. These conditions tend to be realized when all externalities are internalized and the cost of capital is determined in competitive markets.[4] We have seen that the aim of maximizing pure economic rent also requires the internalization of externalities and price determination in competitive markets. The same conditions that tend to maximize pure economic rent are the conditions that tend to maximize the value of land to society.

[4] Probably most economists would agree that the social rate of discount is that which equates the marginal product of capital with the marginal rate of time preference. This tends to be the private rate of discount also under the conditions itemized. However, in a world of imperfect markets and a corporation income tax that drives a wedge between the marginal product of capital and the marginal rate of time preference, it is difficult even to define the social rate of discount in a way that most economists would agree upon. We can make no contribution to the solution of this problem. We can only note its existence and acknowledge that it qualifies the proposition that under competitive bidding by private firms the private value of land tends to equal its social value. For a cogent discussion of the discount rate problem, see Talbot Page, *Conservation and Economic Efficiency: An Approach to Materials Policy* (Baltimore, Md., Johns Hopkins Press for Resources for the Future, 1977) pp. 145–173.

One concluding observation can be made here. Pure economic rent, as we have seen, is a surplus. It is an income over and above that necessary to call forth the services of a factor of production such as land. As such, it is an ideal source of revenue to government. It can be absorbed entirely by government without reducing the nation's output of goods and services. To the extent that government receives this form of income from the leasing of land, it can reduce taxes that would fall, directly or indirectly, on those incomes necessary to call forth production and would, therefore, to some extent, inhibit production. Thus, seen in another way, a policy of leasing land under terms and conditions that tend to maximize pure economic rent is a policy that tends to enhance social welfare.

Accordingly, we conclude that government leasing of lands for minerals production should be guided by the aim of maximizing the present value of pure economic rent from such lands. We focus on rent rather than directly on the general welfare that should be enhanced, because rent is the central element in the leasing agreement and is the immediate, visible consequence of land leasing. But we must not lose sight of the more fundamental objective of maximizing welfare.

4

The Relevant Economics—
Efficient Extraction of Minerals
and Environmental Protection

THE EFFICIENT EXTRACTION OF MINERALS

Thus far we have simply assumed that in connection with the determination of rent the extraction of minerals is economically efficient. Now we must examine the matter more closely.[1] Minerals extraction has a unique characteristic, the implications of which are most important for our purposes. We shall spell these out and show that, particularly in the case of oil and gas, competition in extraction does not necessarily assure economic efficiency. We shall show that in the interest of maximizing pure economic rent some degree of regulation may be required.

THE TIME-DISTRIBUTION OF EXTRACTION

Minerals extraction differs from most other productive processes in that the minerals physically available, in specific deposits and in total within a geographic area, are limited in amount and are nonrenewable; that is, extraction implies depletion of the mineral resource. Depletion, in turn, implies at least the possibility of ultimate exhaustion in some

---

[1] This chapter relies heavily on Stephen L. McDonald, *Petroleum Conservation in the United States* (Baltimore, Md., Johns Hopkins University Press for Resources for the Future, 1971) chap. 5.

sense. Whereas agriculture, for instance, can be continued indefinitely on a parcel of land with, if necessary, purely organic means of maintaining soil fertility, the extraction of minerals from a parcel of land must inevitably some day cease because depletion of the mineral deposit must in time reach the point where further extraction is uneconomic. We can imagine in some instances the total physical exhaustion of a mineral deposit, but ordinarily extraction ceases because seams become so thin, reservoir pressures become so low, or ores become so lean that further extraction will not pay for itself.

Since the total amount of a mineral in a deposit is limited, most relevantly in an economic sense, the operator cannot choose a rate of extraction and maintain it indefinitely. Additional production in one period, moreover, implies reduced production in another period and, perhaps, a shorter time to abandonment. Given these constraints, a key decision of the operator is the *distribution* of extraction over time. To him a major dimension of the problem of efficient production is the time-distribution of extraction.

To explain, we begin with the proposition that the owner of the right to extract a mineral from a given parcel of land, say, a lessee, rationally seeks to maximize at a given time, time zero, the present value of his property. That is, at the outset the lessee seeks to maximize V_o in Equation 4-1.

$$V_o = -I_o + \frac{(R - C)_1}{(1 + r)^1} + \frac{(R - C)_2}{(1 + r)^2} + \ldots \frac{(R - C)_n}{(1 + r)^n} \qquad (4\text{-}1)$$

where V_o = present value at time zero
I_o = initial investment outlay
R = cash revenue in the indicated periods
C = cash costs in the indicated periods
r = the rate of discount
n = the expected year of abandonment

Or, once the initial investment is sunk and what was time one has become time zero, the lessee seeks to maximize V_o' in Equation 4-2:

$$V_o' = (R - C)_o + \frac{(R - C)_1}{(1 + r)^1} + \frac{(R - C)_2}{(1 + r)^2} + \ldots \frac{(R + C)_n}{(1 + r)^n} \qquad (4\text{-}2)$$

Assume, for the moment, that the initial investment is sunk, and define net revenue as $R - C$. Further, define marginal net revenue

(MNR) as marginal revenue minus marginal cost ($MR - MC$), or the increment to net revenue that results from a small increment to output. It is readily apparent that the necessary condition of maximizing Equation 4-2 is the equating of discounted MNRs in all periods. That is, for Equation 4-2 to be maximized the following equality must hold $MNR_o = MNR_1/(1+r)^1 = MNR_2/(1+r)^2 = \ldots MNR_n/(1+r)^n$. When this condition holds, the minerals producer cannot transfer a unit of output from one period to another without incurring a sacrifice equal in value to his gain.

What assures that a producer can bring about through his own actions the equation of MNRs in all periods? Why does the maximization of value not require all production to be concentrated in time zero? Assume a producer of minerals on a given parcel of land whose capacity is limited by his (sunk) initial investment. Assume that he is one of many such producers, so that his output decisions in any period do not affect price, hence marginal revenue. Finally, assume an initial, tentative plan of extraction over time so that $MNR_o > MNR_1/(1+r)^1 > \ldots MNR_n/(1+r)^n$. Clearly, the operator can increase the value of his property by accelerating planned depletion, thereby in effect transferring units of output from the future toward the present. As he does so, his planned output in periods to which output is transferred more closely approaches capacity, while that in periods from which output is transferred falls relative to capacity. At some point marginal costs in the former periods must rise, while those in the latter periods must fall. Rising marginal cost means declining MNR, and falling marginal cost means increasing MNR. Consequently, the original inequality of MNRs in different periods steadily diminishes as planned output is transferred toward the present, and eventually it must disappear. When it disappears, the operator has achieved the value-maximizing planned time-distribution of extraction subject to the constraint imposed by capacity.

The maximization of present value is the equivalent of maximizing profit in each period, which requires the equating of marginal revenue with marginal cost. At any given time, say, time zero, marginal cost takes two forms. The first is marginal cost directly associated with production in that period, MC_o, which we shall call marginal operating cost. The second is the present value of the marginal net revenue sacrificed in future by virtue of an additional unit of present output, $MNR_t/(1+r)^t$, which we shall call the marginal user cost of timing. Now when $MNR_o = MNR_t/(1+r)^t$, then $MR_o - MC_o - MNR_t/(1+r)^t = 0$; which is to say, marginal revenue minus marginal operating cost minus marginal user cost of timing equals zero, or marginal revenue minus (total) marginal cost equals zero, the indicated condition for maximizing profit.

The value-maximizing—that is, efficient—time-distribution for the individual operator is also efficient from a social point of view, provided that there are no uninternalized externalities and that the prices involved, including the discount rate, are determined in competitive markets. A socially efficient time-distribution of extraction and use of a depletable resource is what is rationally meant by "conservation" of such a resource.

In connection with the equating of MNRs by the process described above, we may note that bottlenecks, say, in transportation, may limit the growth of revenues as output is transferred to a given period, so that MNR falls all the more rapidly in that period. This effect, also, may facilitate the equating of MNRs in different periods. But if bottlenecks are present which could in a social sense profitably be eliminated, the thus constrained time-distribution of minerals extraction is not socially efficient.

In any case, what is perceived as an efficient time-distribution of extraction at one time may be perceived as inefficient under different circumstances. What we have called *the* value-maximizing planned time-distribution of extraction by the assumed operator obviously depends on a given set of present and expected prices and costs, and a given rate of discount. A rise in expected future prices or a fall in expected future costs relative to present ones would induce a shift in the planned time-distribution of extraction toward the future. Similarly, a fall in the discount rate, reflecting, say, a fall in the market rate of interest, would induce a redistribution of output in the direction of the future. And reverse changes would induce a redistribution of output toward the present. In short, the value-maximizing (efficient) time-distribution of extraction changes with every change in the discount rate and present and expected prices and costs. The operator must continually "track" the efficient plan of output as depletion progresses, events unfold, and circumstances change.

Equation 4-2 may also be employed to throw light on the abandonment decision. If the operator has no salvageable capital equipment, abandonment occurs when variable costs have risen to a level equal to price. Short of that point, each additional unit of extraction adds something to profits. But if the operator has some salvageable capital equipment, as is usually the case, abandonment occurs earlier. It occurs when the present value of expected net revenues has fallen to equality with the net market value of the salvageable equipment; that is, when:

$$V'_o = S_o = (R - C)_o + \frac{(R - C)_1}{(1 + r)^1} + \dots \frac{(R - C)_n}{(1 + r)^n} \qquad (4\text{-}3)$$

where S is salvage value net of salvage costs and time zero is the time of decision. Production beyond that point adds less to the present worth of the operator than the alternative use or sale of the salvageable equipment. The appropriate time of abandonment is also a part of the efficiency problem.

We have assumed to this point that capacity is limited by a sunk initial investment. We must now relax this assumption and entertain the possibility that capacity can be increased by an additional investment in shafts, wells, equipment, and so forth. If so, marginal costs in different periods will be affected, and the efficient time-distribution of extraction will be changed. Generally, up to a point, additional present capacity shifts the value-maximizing time-distribution of extraction toward the present.

Figure 4-1 illustrates the effect of additional capacity on marginal costs. Adding to capacity shifts the marginal cost schedule in any period in the same direction as capacity, as from MC_o to MC_1, so that at any rate of output, say, OA, marginal costs are lowered. If they are lowered by the same amount in all periods, or possibly more in earlier periods, then MNR_o will rise relative to $MNR_t/(1+r)^t$, where t denotes some future period, and a redistribution of extraction toward the present will be induced. This redistribution continues until MNR_o once again equals $MNR_t/(1+r)^t$, and present value of expected net revenues is once again maximized.

The new maximum present value of expected net revenues will be different, in all likelihood, from the original one. Let us suppose it is higher. If the gain in maximum present value is larger than the incremental investment allowing it, then the latter will have proved to be profitable; it will have added something to the present value of the property. Further increments to investment may also be profitable; but at some point the gain in maximum present value of net revenues must

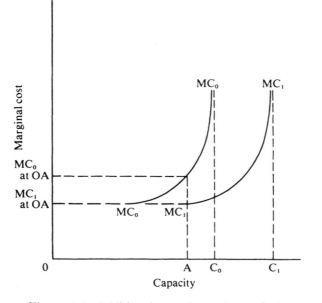

Figure 4-1. Additional capacity and marginal costs. [Figure is based on figure 6 in Stephen L. McDonald, *Petroleum Conservation in the United States: An Economic Analysis* (Baltimore, Md., Johns Hopkins University Press for Resources for the Future, 1971) page 81.]

equal and then fall below the incremental investment, due to diminishing returns at the margin as more and more capital is combined with a fixed amount of land. Where gain in maximum present value just equals incremental investment, the present value of the property V_o, in Equation 4-1, is maximized. This point defines simultaneously the optimum (most efficient) capacity and the optimum time-distribution of extraction.

When V_o is maximized, the pure economic rent generated is also maximized. As explained earlier, if prospective lessees are numerous and knowledgeable, they will tend to bid V_o, as a lease bonus or its equivalent in periodic rent payments, for the privilege of extracting minerals from the land in question. Terms and conditions of leasing that facilitate optimization of capacity and time-distribution of extraction are terms and conditions conducive to maximization of pure economic rent.

THE SPECIAL CASE OF OIL AND GAS PRODUCTION

Optimizing capacity and the time-distribution of oil and gas extraction involves three considerations not relevant to the extraction of hard (nonliquid) minerals. The first consideration is that in many situations the volume of oil (and sometimes gas) ultimately recoverable from a reservoir is inversely related to the speed at which extraction is attempted. The second consideration is that where there are two or more operators extracting oil or gas from the same reservoir, those extracting at a higher rate than their neighbors do so partly at the expense of the latter by inducing a flow of oil or gas across property lines within the reservoir. The third consideration is that gas is commonly found in association with oil in natural reservoirs, and that the efficiency of oil recovery may depend on whether the gas is produced simultaneously with the oil or retained in the reservoir until all recoverable oil is extracted. These three unique characteristics of oil and gas production largely account for the problem of oil and gas conservation, and as we shall see, the approach to dealing with them is highly relevant to the matter of maximizing the pure economic rent that is derivable from lands containing such minerals.

Oil and gas are found under pressure in subsurface strata of permeable rock so distorted and over- and underlain by impermeable materials as to trap otherwise migrant particles of the minerals and form natural reservoirs. Having marine origins in early geological ages, oil and gas are nearly always associated with (saline) water, which, being heavier, lies below them in the reservoir. Gas, when associated with oil, may be partly or wholly dissolved in the oil, with the undissolved gas lying on top of the oil to form a "cap."

When wells tap a reservoir, the difference in pressure between the reservoir and the bottom of the well bores causes the fluids to flow into the latter and thence to the surface. If the wells tap the oil zone only, oil and dissolved gas flow only into the well bores at first; with the gas cap above, if any, expanding, and the water below advancing, primarily through recharge (being little compressible), to occupy the space in the reservoir vacated by the oil. If the oil is withdrawn slowly enough, gravity maintains a regular, horizontal interface between the remaining oil and the water below, and between the oil and the gas above. In such a situation the water and gas seem to act like pistons, "driving" the oil before them toward the wells. Depending on the dominant source of expansive pressure, the reservoir is said to have a water or a gas-cap "drive." A third type of drive is the expansive pressure of compressed gas dissolved in oil—a dissolved-gas drive. All three drives may be active at some time in a given reservoir.

If the oil is withdrawn rapidly enough, however, gravity cannot maintain a regular, horizontal interface between the oil and the other fluids; the water and gas tend to advance irregularly, forming flow channels directly to the wells in the reservoir and bypassing pockets of oil that may never be economically recoverable. Moreover, the escape of water and gas into wells results in a more rapid depletion of pressure in the reservoir, so that the point is reached sooner where pressure differential is not sufficient to maintain economical production. Even where artificial lift, as by pumps, is employed, the necessity to lift and dispose of large quantities of saltwater tends to limit the economic life and ultimate recovery of oil from the reservoirs. Thus, beyond some critical point, increasing the rate of extraction steadily decreases the amount of oil ultimately recoverable. The critical rate of extraction is known in the industry as the *maximum efficient rate* (MER).[2]

The MER concept applies most directly to water- or gas-cap drives, for the reasons indicated above. There is no MER in the case of a reservoir operating on a pure dissolved-gas drive. However, when reservoir pressure is sufficiently reduced for the gas to come out of solution, restrained production of oil may facilitate the formation of a gas cap, so that thereafter there is a gas-cap drive and a MER for the reservoir.

It should be noted also that where there is a gas cap, the production of gas simultaneously with oil—as against retaining the gas in the reservoir—speeds the depletion of the reservoir pressure and may reduce the ultimate recovery of oil. If there is an alternative water drive present, the depletion of pressure with removal of gas may lower the rate of oil extraction that is consistent with maintaining a regular interface between oil and water. Where there is no alternative water drive, the depletion of gas pressure obviously accelerates abandonment and reduces the amount of oil that is ultimately recoverable.

The expulsive mechanism in the case of nonassociated gas reservoirs, or gas-cap oil reservoirs after the oil is effectively depleted and the gas is finally to be recovered, is simply the expansion of gas, as pressure is

---

[2] See Stuart E. Buckley, ed., *Petroleum Conservation* (Dallas, American Institute of Mining and Metallurgical Engineers, 1951) pp. 151–152.

released by one or more well bores. The MER concept does not apply here in the usual way. Indeed, in a nonassociated gas reservoir with water drive, ultimate recovery of gas may be increased by speeding up the rate of withdrawal. The reason for this is that with rapid extraction of gas and corresponding reduction of pressure, expanding water traps and makes unrecoverable fewer molecules of gas; whereas with a slow drop in pressure, expanding water traps gas under greater compression, hence greater concentration of molecules.

Oil and gas would, of course, not be producible if they (and water) could not flow through connected pore spaces of the host rock. But being so mobile, they can move in response to pressure differentials across property lines in the reservoir where there are two or more operators with extraction rights. The operator who extracts oil or gas more rapidly reduces relative pressure in the neighborhood of his wells and causes fluids to migrate toward them from other parts of the reservoir. Particularly if the wells are close to property lines, they can, in effect, produce oil or gas at the expense of the neighbor's wells. Having no other recourse at law, which rests on the "rule of capture."[3] the neighbors can protect themselves only by producing at a faster rate also. Thus where there is competitive extraction from a reservoir, unrestrained by regulation, the overall rate of extraction tends to be so high from the outset that the MER is exceeded and ultimate recovery reduced.

Let us now apply these principles to the problem of maximizing the value of an oil or gas property, hence maximizing pure economic rent therefrom. Suppose, to begin with, that there is only one operator in a reservoir who has the sole right to extract the oil and gas. Let the operator have an initial, tentative investment in wells, so that the problem is one of maximizing the present value of expected net revenues from extraction. As with any mineral operator, our operator seeks to maximize V'_o, in Equation 4-2. This requires that:

$$MNR_o = (1 + b_1) \frac{MNR_1}{(1 + r)^1} = \ldots (1 + b_n) \frac{MNR_n}{(1 + r)^n} \qquad (4\text{-}4)$$

---

[3] According to the rule of capture, oil or gas belongs to the operator who recovers it through his wells, regardless of where the minerals may have originated in the reservoir. The key court cases in the development of the rule are: *Westmoreland and Cambria Natural Gas Co.* v. *Dewitt*, 130 Pa. 235, 18 Atl. 72d (1889); *Kelly* v. *Ohio Oil Co.*, 57 O.S. 317 (1897); and *Barnard* v. *Monogahela Natural Gas Co.*, 216 Pa. 362, 365, 65 Atl. 801, 802 (1907).

where $MNR_1 \ldots n = $ the net revenue lost in the period indicated from the unit successfully transferred to the present

$b_1 \ldots n = $ the fraction of a unit of oil or gas additionally lost from recovery in the period indicated by virtue of transferring one unit of production from that period to the present.

Now we must consider that when an operator succeeds in increasing present production by, say, one barrel of oil, he forgoes in some future period not only the alternative net revenues that barrel would have returned, but possibly in addition the net revenues from a fraction of a barrel that consequently cannot be recovered in that future period. In other words, an additional barrel today costs him $(1 + b_t)$ barrels tomorrow, where b_t may be greater than zero. Where today's rate of production is equal to or less than the MER, by definition of the latter, b_t is zero, and an additional barrel today costs as much as a barrel tomorrow.

Accordingly, the oil and gas operator seeking to maximize the present value of net revenues has potentially an additional restraint on current production. The more sensitive b_t is to the current rate of production, the more restrained is the latter, ceteris paribus. This does not mean, however, that the value-maximizing operator will always choose the present rate of extraction that makes b_t zero. If present prices (costs) are sufficiently high (low) relative to expected future ones, or if the rate of discount is sufficiently high, the value-maximizing time-distribution of extraction may involve some voluntary loss of ultimate recovery. In this case the loss of ultimate recovery is outweighed in value by the interest saved by virtue of accelerated recovery of some barrels. Note that the lone operator's loss of ultimate recovery is the same as society's; so that on this account the operator is induced to select the same time-distribution as would society, the latter acting presumably through a conservation commission.

In an oil or gas reservoir the number of wells limits capacity at a given time. Given the number of wells, the present value of expected net revenues behaves with respect to current output, as indicated by the curve *PV* in figure 4-2. At first, as the present rate of output increases, present value rises because of the lower discount of present relative to future net revenues. But eventually, the constraint of a given number of wells must cause present marginal costs to rise relative to future ones,

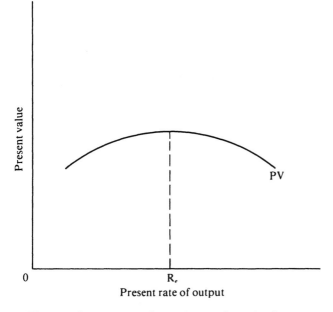

Figure 4-2. Present value and rate of production.

the effect of which outweighs the interest saving of early extraction, so that *PV* falls with further increase in present output. OR_e is the value-maximizing (optimum) rate of output corresponding to the given number of wells.

Increasing the number of wells relaxes the capacity constraint and lowers present marginal costs. With more wells the optimum rate of production may be higher than before. However, at some point, as the rate of present production increases, the effect of reduced ultimate recovery must be felt; and eventually this effect must dominate the effect of interest saving. Consequently, the change in maximum present value, as the number of wells is increased, must equal and then fall below incremental well costs. There is, therefore, some limited number of wells and rate of present output that (in association with planned rates of output) maximizes the present value of the property.

The determination of the optimum number of wells and rate of output is illustrated in figure 4-3. Here the vertical axis measures the net present value of well costs, and the horizontal axis measures the present rate of output. Each curve indicates the behavior of net present value

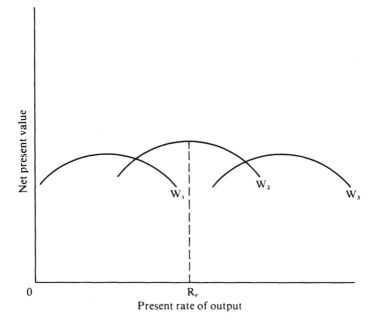

Figure 4-3. Optimum number of wells and rate of output. [Figure is based on figure 7 in Stephen L. McDonald, *Petroleum Conservation in the United States: An Economic Analysis* (Baltimore, Md., Johns Hopkins University Press for Resources for the Future, 1971) page 82.]

with respect to present output, given the number of wells. There is a different curve for each number of wells, W_1, W_2, and so forth. Where the maximum net present value is achieved is determined by the optimum number of wells (W_2) and the optimum present rate of output (OR_e). The optimum number of wells and optimum rate of output are limited not only by diminishing returns, as capital invested rises relative to the input of land, but also by the tendency of ultimate recovery to decline as the present rate of output is increased. Beyond W_2 these two effects dominate interest saving.

Again, the private optima of the lone operator are the social optima also if prices, costs, and rate of discount are determined in competitive markets, and there are no uninternalized externalities.

Consider, now, the case in which there are two or more competitive operators working an oil or gas reservoir. Each tries to maximize the present value of his separate property (lease), and each must now consider that by adopting a production rate higher than that of the neighbors oil or gas will flow from their property to his (or that by adopting a lower rate of production than one's neighbors he allows them to induce a flow across property lines at his expense). With a given number of wells, maximization of present value of net revenues now requires that:

$$MNR_o = (1 - X_1)(1 + b_1)\frac{MNR_1}{(1 + r)^1} = \ldots (1 - X_n)(1 + b_n)\frac{MNR_n}{(1 + r)^n}$$

$$(4\text{-}5)$$

where $X_1 \ldots n$ is the fraction of a barrel (or MCF) lost to a neighbor by virtue of postponing the production of a barrel to the period indicated. Clearly, X_t acts as a negative restraint in current production. The net revenues lost in the future, as the result of successfully transferring a unit of production from future to present, are smaller than in the case of the lone operator of a reservoir. Therefore, the value-maximizing time-distribution of extraction in the present case will involve relatively more early extraction than in the case of the lone operator. There will be less ultimate recovery from the reservoir, but such a loss may mean nothing to the individual operator if he can sufficiently compensate himself by producing through his own wells oil or gas attracted from the property of others.

The competitive operator will also drill more wells per unit of land than will the lone operator. This is because the return to the incremental well now includes additional oil that may be attracted from neighboring properties. Given the negative factor X_t, the perceived effect of declining ultimate recovery is weaker and does not as quickly make the gain in maximum present value fall below incremental well cost, as additional wells are drilled and extraction is accelerated. In figure 4-3, the maximum net present value associated with, say, W_3 appears higher than that associated with W_2, so that W_3, rather than W_2, appears to be the optimum number of wells. Since all operators can play the game, the result is greatly accelerated production, an excessive investment in wells, and high loss of ultimate recovery (high b).

The third problem is one that arises from combination oil and gas reservoirs, where gas is both a product to be extracted and sold as well as being an agent of efficient extraction of oil. Assume a reservoir of the classic anticlinal type, illustrated schematically in figure 4-4. A gas cap

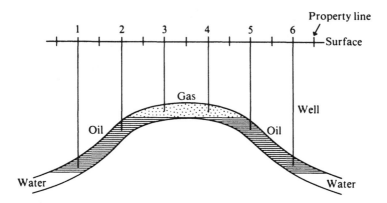

Figure 4-4. An anticlinal trap with oil and gas.

lies on top of the oil in the reservoir, but because of the slope of the trap wells, drilled vertically from the center of leases on the surface, can generally tap either the oil zone or the gas zone but not both. The problem is whether to extract gas through wells 3 and 4 concurrently with extraction of oil through the other wells, or to retain the gas in the reservoir as a device of pressure maintenance until the oil is depleted before recovering the gas (which will then have expanded into the original oil zone).

If there were a lone operator in the reservoir, he would simply compare the present values of two alternative streams of net revenue. In the first, both oil and gas revenues are received from the outset, and the stream would be shortened by the relatively early depletion of reservoir pressures and the leaving of some otherwise recoverable oil in the reservoir. In the second, only oil revenues are received at first, the stream of such revenues being long, while gas revenues are received only at the end. The operator would choose the plan that promised the highest present value. Obviously, the choice of plan depends on the efficiency of the gas-cap drive (perhaps in combination with a water drive) in producing the oil, and on the present and future prices of oil and gas, as well as on the costs of production. It might also be dependent on the rate of discount if the time shapes of revenues in the two plans are substantially different. For example, if the water drive is dominant and the gas cap adds little to oil-recovery efficiency, the first plan might be economically superior. For another, if gas prices are expected to rise continually in the future while oil prices remain constant or decline, the second plan might yield the higher present value. In any case, the operator would be free to choose the economically superior plan (and to change it later if circumstances change), and the rent he would offer for extraction rights would reflect the expected results.

But suppose instead that there are many lessees competing for the minerals in the common reservoir, each one on a separate property unit overlying the reservoir. The owners of wells 3 and 4 can produce only gas, while the owners of wells 1, 2, 5, and 6 can produce only oil. In this case there could be only one operating scheme: the concurrent production of oil and gas. The owners of wells 3 and 4 could not afford to wait until the oil was depleted to recover their gas; and besides, if they did wait, the gas area would have expanded into the original oil zone and the owners of wells 1, 2, 5, and 6 would then be able to extract for themselves part of the gas. If the concurrent production of oil and gas yields less present value to the operators as a whole than the alternative scheme, then the economic rent generated would be less than the pure economic rent available. A group of competitive operators, knowing they might have to "select" a poor plan, would bid less in the aggregate for extraction rights than would a lone operator, adequately financed, who knew he would be free to choose the optimum plan depending on circumstances to be discovered.

It should now be clear that competitive extraction of oil and gas from common reservoirs is not conducive to maximizing present value from a social point of view, nor is it conducive to maximizing pure economic rent from the lands involved. Where there are two or more operators in a common reservoir, the interest of society and of the government as landlord is best served by eliminating the otherwise resulting competition within the reservoir while retaining it in the industry as a whole. This may be done in either of two general ways. The first is to restrain competition by regulation within reservoirs. The second is to require the operation of reservoirs as units.

Restraining competition by regulation is the approach taken generally by the states on the lands subject to their jurisdiction;[4] and the federal government has taken a similar approach on its lands, largely imitating the regulation of states in which, or contiguous to which, the federal lands are located. Under these regulations, well density is limited, and the rate of production from each reservoir is limited to the MER or to

---

[4] For a full discussion, see McDonald, *Petroleum Conservation*.

that reservoir's share of the statewide market demand, as given by a basic schedule relating well allowables to depth and acreage. Reservoir allowables are then allocated to wells on some presumably equitable basis. While this approach to regulation controls the private and social wastes of excessive well drilling and the loss of ultimate recovery, it does not assure that each reservoir is developed and operated in such a way as to maximize its present value. In order to be administratively feasible the system has to be based on a few uniform rules, schedules, and the like, and there is no attempt by the regulators to adjust to a change in expected prices and costs or to a changing discount rate. Where there is conflict over the proper handling of associated gas, the approach is to protect the correlative rights of the interested parties rather than to require a value-maximizing plan of operation. Regulation of the sort described is undoubtedly helpful, but it is not conducive to maximum pure economic rent on the affected lands.

The alternative to this is compulsory unitization.[5] Unitization means the pooling of property interests within a reservoir, agreement on an equitable division of net revenues from the reservoir as a whole, and the creation of a single management in order to plan and conduct extractive operations in the reservoir which is to be treated as a single unit rather than as a collection of competing leases. A unit may be formed prospectively by a group of lessees planning exploration in an area that is believed to be promising, each lessee having a commitment to the plan if the land is within the productive area; or a unit may be formed after the productive area has been discovered. Most purely voluntary units are formed to facilitate secondary recovery operations. In any case, the central purpose of unitization is to remove the motivation of individual lessees to drill wells and select production rates designed to gain oil or gas at the expense of neighboring lessees. It removes X from the condition of maximizing present value. In short—particularly if it occurs early enough in the life of a reservoir—it allows the operators as a whole to select that well density and time-distribution of extraction which promises to maximize the value of the reservoir to them (and incidentally to society). It is sufficiently flexible to permit the time-distribution of extraction to be changed with a change in the discount rate and expected prices and costs relative to present ones. It permits the value-maximizing use of gas found in association with oil. And it

[5] Ibid., chap. 10.

protects property interests directly in the agreement to share net revenues. In general, by facilitating the value-maximizing plan of development and recovery from a reservoir, unitization tends to maximize the pure economic rent derivable from the land involved.

Unitization is often difficult to accomplish voluntarily in the case of large reservoirs on private lands, due to the many, diverse property interests present. But where government is the only landlord and there are few operator-lessees, as on the outer continental shelf, voluntary unitization is simpler and compulsory unitization less likely to be strongly resisted.

In passing, it may be observed that the size of the typical lease has a bearing on the problem under discussion. Where leases are small, there are likely to be many property interests, lessors, and lessees in reservoirs of given size; and unitization is relatively difficult to carry out. But where leases are large, as on the outer continental shelf, in some instances there will be only one lessee in a reservoir, and in others only a few. Thus large leases, ceteris paribus, tend to reduce the problems associated with competitive extraction from common reservoirs.

UNITIZATION IN THE CASE OF HARD MINERALS

As the foregoing suggests, hard minerals do not share those properties of oil and gas that make ultimate recovery depend on the rate of extraction, and that make competitive extraction inconsistent with maximizing present value from a social point of view. Generally, therefore, the extraction of hard minerals need not be regulated, and unitization of separate leases in a common deposit would serve no useful purpose. However, it is possible to imagine situations in which leases are too small to allow efficient hard mineral extraction because of even the minimum investment that must be made in shafts, equipment, and perhaps transportation facilities. In such cases it may be profitable, both privately and socially, to pool separate leases in order to form an economical unit; and since the separate leases may be exploited sequentially in an efficient plan of extraction, rather than all at once, it may be essential to have a scheme of net revenue sharing similar to those employed in oil and gas units. Where the option to form beneficial units is present, lessees would tend to bid more for extraction rights, and the rent offered in the aggregate would tend to approach more closely the pure economic rent. Thus, in general, but especially in the case of oil and gas extraction, unitization tends to maximize the pure economic rent derivable from lands containing minerals.

ENVIRONMENTAL PROTECTION

In chapter 3 it was explained that maximization of pure economic rent from federal mineral lands requires, among other things, the internalization of external costs such as environmental damage; that is, regulation should cause such costs to be borne in the first instance by the firms responsible for them so that they are ultimately reflected in the prices of the firms' products. Such internalization raises product prices and reduces leasing revenues, but it tends to restrict revenues to the true surplus in minerals production, to reduce environmental damage, and to increase welfare. Our purpose in the present chapter is to expand on the problem of reducing environmental damage through internalization of costs.

MAJOR TYPES OF ENVIRONMENTAL DAMAGE IN MINERALS PRODUCTION

It will not be possible to describe all the types of environmental damage that may occur in connection with minerals production, but the following major types may be identified as indicative of the range.

Contamination of Freshwater-bearing Strata in Oil Well Drilling and Abandonment. As wells are sunk in the search for oil and gas, the hole ordinarily passes through freshwater-bearing strata at relatively shallow levels, then saltwater-bearing strata at the greater depths. The saltwater (often several times as concentrated as seawater) being under greater pressure, tends to enter the well bore, rise toward the surface and invade the freshwater-bearing strata, contaminating the water therein. It may be prevented from doing so during drilling by the pressure of drilling fluid ("mud"), and in preparing a well for production or abandonment, by appropriate casing and plugs. Surface damage from saltwater flowing out of the well may be prevented by similar means.

Contamination of Surface Soil and Water in Disposing of Waste Brines in Oil Production. Oil and gas are nearly always found in association with saltwater, and substantial amounts of such water, along with minerals, may be conducted to the surface. There it must be separated and disposed of. If dumped into leaky evaporation pits or surface drainage systems, it commonly causes damage to soil, water, plant life, and animals. It may be safely disposed of, although at greater expense, by reinjecting it into the stratum from which it came. Saltwater from offshore wells may often be safely disposed of in the surrounding sea.

Oil Spills from Offshore Wells. Oil spilled into the water around offshore wells tends to become widely dispersed and to be carried often by wind and tide long distances to shallow bays and shores, where it contaminates fisheries, other wildlife habitats, and recreational beaches. While the damage may be temporary and susceptible to various clean-up techniques, it can be costly to a number of economic interests, from oystermen to bathers. It can be controlled by devices ranging from appropriate emergency equipment on wells to due care in transferring oil from platform to barge.

Destruction of Land Surface in Strip-mining Coal. When coal is strip-mined, topsoil and immediate subsoil are stripped away by draglines and piled aside so that access to the coal may be had by similar machinery. If no restorative action is taken upon removal of the coal, open pits and eroding piles of soil remain as hazards to persons and livestock, threats to surrounding soil and streams, and blotches on otherwise scenic beauty. In places where the land is level, pits may be refilled, topsoil restored, and grass or timber cover reestablished—at some expense, of course. On mountainsides, however, restoration may be unfeasible and permanent damage may occur not only to scenery and forest, but also to farms and residences in the path of erosion.

Surface Subsidence over Coal Mines and Oil Fields. The removal of underground fluids in oil fields occasionally results in collapse of the producing stratum and subsidence of the surface over the field. The result can be destruction of buildings, roads, and other improvements, and possible flooding if the area is adjacent to water. Similar effects can flow from the collapse of supports in underground coal mines, due to age or original inadequacy. Subsidence over oil fields can be prevented by reinjection of fluids (water) to maintain pressure, and over coal mines by provision of permanent pillars (for example, concrete or unmined coal) properly sized and spaced.

Damage to Land Values Through Disposal of Spent Oil Shale. The shale is mined, crushed, and retorted in order to extract the shale oil. The residual material, or spent shale, from the retorting process has a greater volume than the original shale. There is, therefore, a substantial disposal problem. It cannot all be returned to the original site, partly because an area must be kept clear for ongoing mining operations. It must therefore be dumped in the surrounding area, where it may be destructive of scenery, wildlife habitat, and stream systems. The spent shale may be carried into the air, or toxic minerals may be leached into streams. There is no entirely damage-free way of disposing of spent oil shale, but some disposal sites may be more acceptable than others, and mining should be restricted to such areas.[6]

THE DESIRABILITY OF INTERNALIZATION

There are at least two ways in which the question of the desirability of internalizing external costs may be viewed. In the first, the environment may be viewed as producing certain amenities of value to man. These amenities are a part of the social product that represents our collective income, the latter in its most fundamental form being a flow of human satisfactions. The production of minerals (or other goods) may, in ways suggested above, interfere with the production of environmental amenities and thus add less to the total social product than the value of the minerals themselves. In other words, the production of minerals may involve not only the usual labor and capital costs of extraction, but, in addition, a sacrifice of other valuable "goods." Beyond some point society becomes worse off, as when minerals production expands, or in other situations where the incremental value of minerals may be less than the incremental cost. This way of viewing the matter suggests a tradeoff between ordinary goods and environmental amenities and some optimum combination of their output. In the optimum combination the production of ordinary goods such as minerals would be pushed to the point where incremental value just equals in-

---

[6] The author is indebted to Patrick H. Geehan for the following comment: "Volume expansion [in shale retorting] is not a problem if associated mineral values are present and extracted. [Spent shale] can be returned to underground mines. Depending on the retort process, the spent shale may not become airborne."

cremental cost, including the sacrifice of amenities. Producers of minerals would voluntarily check output at this point only if they had to bear in the first instance the costs of environmental damages.

The other way of viewing the matter leads to the same conclusion, but it involves a slightly different emphasis. In this way, the production of specific goods by specific firms is viewed as involving specific costs. Certain costs, such as the employment of labor and capital, are ordinarily borne in the first instance by the firms in question and may be termed *internal costs*. Other costs, such as environmental damage, however, are ordinarily borne by entities external to the firms in question and do not thus enter the costs that must be covered by the prices paid by consumers. The total of internal and external costs is the total *social* cost of the goods being produced; this is what society really pays to get the goods. From the firm's point of view, the optimum output of goods corresponds to the point where incremental value (price) is equal to incremental *internal* cost. From the point of view of society, it is where incremental value is equal to incremental *social* (internal *plus* external) cost. If there are incremental external costs, therefore, private firms tend to push the output of the relevant goods too far; that is, beyond the point that maximizes net benefits to society. Too many such goods are produced, and too much environmental damage is done. The appropriate amount of goods would be produced only if external costs are internalized, which is to say, if they become a part of the firm's internal costs.

The first view emphasizes the proposition that ordinary goods and environmental amenities are alternatives; and that to have more of the one we must accept less of the other. The second view emphasizes the proposition that reduction of environmental amenities in association with the production of a good is a part of the cost of producing that good which ought to be reflected with other costs in the price of the good. Although the emphasis is different, these views are in harmony; they imply the same thing. Both lead to the conclusion that to the extent we rely upon the price system to govern the mix of goods produced, external costs such as environmental damage should be internalized.

It is important to point out that in neither view is it the social purpose to protect the environment per se. The purpose is to maximize human welfare. From neither point of view is it asserted that environmental damages should be completely avoided at all cost. Rather it is

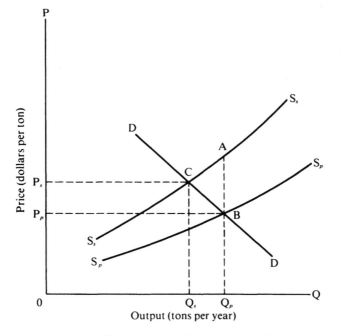

Figure 4-5. Effect of internalizing externalities.

maintained that environmental damages, which in the sense of environmental alteration are involved in the production of almost any ordinary good, whether houses, corn or coal, should be reflected in the prices we pay for what we do produce. This tends to reduce environmental damage by discouraging the consumption of goods whose production causes it, but it may not eliminate the damage altogether.

The principle involved is illustrated in figure 4-5. The price of the good in question is measured on the vertical axis, the quantity produced and consumed on the horizontal axis. DD is the demand schedule for the good. S_pS_p is the supply schedule of the industry reflecting only internal costs. (The supply schedule of a competitive industry is the marginal, or incremental, cost schedule of the industry when the schedule is viewed as the price at which different quantities will be offered for sale.) S_sS_s is the social supply schedule reflecting all internal and external costs. If externalities were ignored, the amount of the good produced and sold would be OQ_p, and the price charged would be OP_p. If externalities were internalized, output would be only OQ_s

and price OP_s. Internalization leads to a higher price of the good and less consumption of it (hence less environmental damage). Society is better off with internalization, for the alternative additional production (Q_sQ_p) would be at a greater incremental cost (CA along S_sS_s) than incremental value (CB along DD), involving a net loss to society of the area of the triangle CAB.[7]

To repeat a point made in chapter 3, if externalities in the production of minerals are internalized, the lands involved will yield less nominal rent; for private long-run costs will be higher and prospective sales lower. Nonetheless, internalization leads toward maximization of pure economic rent, the genuine social surplus produced by mineral lands. It is this surplus, not nominal rent, that the federal government, as custodian of public lands, should try to maximize. To ignore environmental damage in the interest of maximizing nominal rent is equivalent to levying a tax on environmental amenities; and it can be shown in the manner of figure 4-5, with the roles of S_pS_p and S_sS_s reversed, that a differential tax on a single class of products reduces social welfare, ceteris paribus.

INTERNALIZING EXTERNAL COSTS SUCH AS ENVIRONMENTAL DAMAGE

There are several ways or techniques of internalizing externalities.[8] We shall indicate the major ones, each of which may be preferred in a given case to the others.

Prohibition of the Production of the Good Involving the Externality. Strip-mining coal on mountainsides or offshore oil drilling in certain areas might be prohibited. This is obviously the most extreme measure, implying perhaps the inadequacy of other measures. Prohibition, or other measures having the same effect, suggests a situation in which at a price covering all social costs the quantity demanded would be zero.

---

[7] We ignore here the resource costs of internalizing externalities (administration, enforcement), assuming that they would be borne by the public at large like other costs of general government.

[8] Compare with Otto A. David and Morton L. Kamien, "Externalities, Information, and Alternative Collective Action," in Robert Dorfman and Nancy S. Dorfman, eds., *Economics of the Environment* (New York, Norton, 1972) pp. 77–86.

Prevention of the Condition or Event Incident to Production Causing the Externality. For example, drillers for oil and gas may be required to case wells sufficiently in order to prevent the contamination of fresh-water strata, or coal miners might be required to leave pillars in underground mines in order to prevent surface subsidence. This technique implies that prevention is less costly than the externality, and perhaps less costly than the compensation of those injured.

Correction of a Condition Otherwise Damaging. Thus strip miners of coal or other minerals may be required to restore overburden and replant grass or trees, as segments of a deposit are mined out. Or offshore oil operators may be required to clean up beaches damaged by oil spills. This device is similar in effect and implications to prevention.

Requirement That Those Injured Be Compensated. For example, landowners in the path of erosion of spoil banks, or of the overflow of saltwater from evaporation pits in oil operations, may be compensated for damages by the firms causing them. In some situations, such as where damages are selective or occasional, compensation may be both an adequate remedy and less costly than prevention.

Taxation of the Activity or Condition Causing Damage. Thus, saltwater-evaporation pits may be taxed, as may the deposit of oil-shale ash in areas of recreational value. Tax receipts may substitute for other local taxes and thus compensate communities experiencing the loss of amenities; or tax receipts may be used to remedy old damages and to provide alternative recreation facilities. Taxes in effect "put a price on" environmental damage and thus discourage it.[9] They may be progressive and effectively limit damages to small amounts. They encourage innovation and alternative devices, such as the reinjection of saltwater in oil operations into original strata.

These several ways of internalizing externalities are not, of course, mutually exclusive. The requirement of overburden restoration under all circumstances may effectively prohibit strip-mining of coal in certain areas. The requirement that offshore oil operators clean up spills may induce sufficient preventive measures. The taxation of damaging activities, like compensation requirements, may lead to preventive measures,

---

[9] See Larry E. Ruff, "The Economic Common Sense of Pollution," in ibid., pp. 13–15.

correction of damages, or effective prohibition of production in certain areas. Furthermore, two or more of the techniques may be used simultaneously, such as devices to prevent oil spills and requirement of cleanup after unpreventable ones.

It should be obvious that precise internalization of externalities requires the measurement of the latter in pecuniary terms. We cannot by compensation, taxation, and the like make private costs coincide with social costs unless we know what external costs, in fact, are. Ideally, we should be able to construct an external cost schedule in each instance, relating such costs to the output of the relevant goods. It is hardly necessary to say that this cannot be done accurately in every case.

It is fairly easy to measure damages where specific property rights and market values exist. Thus, it is not difficult to measure damages in such cases as surface subsidence over coal mines, where houses and streets are destroyed; spillage of saltwater from oil operations, where agricultural land values are reduced; contamination of commercial oyster beds by offshore oil spills, resulting in a reduced harvest; or the destruction of farmsteads by mudslides originating with discarded overburden in mountainside strip mining. It is much more difficult—sometimes even impossible—to measure damages where property rights are general, where markets do not exist, and where damages are intangible. It is, for example, very difficult to make meaningful estimates of damages where the values destroyed relate to scenery, wildlife habitat, and general recreational facilities. It is almost impossible to say what damages will result from the deposit of oil-shale ash in the producible areas, these being arid, relatively uninhabited, and seldom in private ownership.

Yet to the extent that measurements can be made, they must be if we are, in fact, to raise or protect the level of human welfare by internalizing externalities. Environmental protection, by every device at whatever cost, is not what is called for and can be more harmful to welfare than it is helpful. It is the proper costing of goods that we want, not the total avoidance of environmental costs. Sufficiently good measurement—and we emphasize that in many important instances good measurement is possible—will allow us to choose intelligently among internalizing techniques. That is, it will enable us to select those cases where prohibition, prevention, correction, compensation, or taxation most correctly transfers external costs to the firms and industries causing them.

Let us suppose that, at least in many situations, external damages are measurable in pecuniary terms, and that external cost schedules can be constructed, relating such costs to the rate of output of minerals. What is the proper application of this information? Preferably, a schedule of charges or fees would be levied against the firms causing external damages, with these charges directly corresponding to the measure of damage actually done at each level of output. Any firm could avoid some or all charges by ceasing output, by taking action to prevent some or all damage, by correcting some or all damages unavoidably caused, or by compensating those injured. The firm would choose the action, or combination of actions, promising to maximize profits. It would cease operations in situations or in the range of output where incremental costs, including costs of avoidance and residual externality charges, exceeded price. In order to avoid charges it would choose prevention, correction, or compensation up to the point where incremental costs of such action just equaled the incremental charges avoided. It would result in the optimum combination of responses and the optimum rate of output of the mineral in question.

The foregoing suggests that direct regulation prohibiting production, preventing damages, and so forth, is a second-best solution to be resorted to where external costs are only roughly known, or where administrative costs of levying and enforcing precise charges outweigh the benefits gained. These situations may indeed be prevalent, and direct regulation may therefore have a large role to play. Prohibition may be imposed whereby presumption social costs exceed price. Similarly, prevention or correction may rationally be imposed where it is presumed that they cost less than the damages avoided; and compensation may be preferred where prevention or correction appear to cost more than the damages avoided. Taxation without any clear notion of the magnitude and incidence of external costs is perhaps a third-best solution.

5

The Manner and Rate of Land Leasing

Having outlined the law and regulations and developed the relevant economic principles, we will turn now to consideration of major practical matters in land leasing. In this chapter we will consider three general questions. First, on what basis should leases be granted? Should they be granted solely on the basis of competitive bidding, or should the practice continue of granting some leases to the first qualified applicant? Second, how should competitive bidding be conducted? Should it be by sealed bids or by oral auction? Third, at what rate should land be offered for lease? Should lease sales be accelerated sharply as a means of quickly increasing self-sufficiency?

Except where noted by specific subheadings, the discussion pertains to the mineral fuels in general. The assumed objective is the full capture of economic rent.

THE MANNER OF LEASING: COMPETITIVE VERSUS NONCOMPETITIVE

As we explained in chapter 3, the law requires that oil and gas leases on the outer continental shelf, and onshore oil and gas leases on a known geological structure of a producing field, be granted only on the basis of competitive bidding. The only sale of oil-shale leases was by competitive bidding. Since the passage, in August 1976, of the Federal Coal Leasing Amendments Act of 1975,[1] the leasing of coal lands must be by competitive bidding only; preference-right leases growing out of prospecting permits are no longer allowed. That leaves only oil and gas

---

[1] 90 Stat. 1083–1092.

leases of onshore lands not on a known geological structure, which by law must be leased to the first qualified applicant. In the case of lands covered by expired, canceled, relinquished, or terminated prior leases, the first qualified applicant is determined by means of a drawing from among applicants filing within a specified period. A filing fee of $10 per offer, but no bonus, is required. No prospective lessee may submit more than one offer per lease unit (not to exceed 2,560 acres in size). Since most onshore federal lands with oil and gas prospects have been leased one or more times, the drawing method of granting leases is typical for lands not on a known geological structure.

It turns out that a very small percentage of oil and gas leases onshore are granted competitively. In a study of the years 1965–68, covering the states of Colorado, Montana, New Mexico, and Wyoming, it was found that less than 1 percent of leases granted were awarded competitively.[2] The fundamental reason for this low percentage was given in a statement by the Department of the Interior to the authors of the study:

> The [Geological] Survey annually maps thousands of square miles of land, but geological mapping and subsurface projections alone cannot be used to establish "known geological structures." Without the completion of a discovery well capable of producing oil or gas, there is no authority under the Mineral Leasing Act to set aside such lands for competitive leasing. The Survey does not have the resources necessary to perform extensive drilling programs. The geological data used by GS to establish and revise KGS [known geological structure] boundaries of necessity consists primarily of information from wells drilled by the oil and gas industry. The initial areas designated as KGS's are generally small areas in the immediate vicinity of the wildcat discovery well. One well does not provide adequate subsurface geologic data for determining the areal extent and reservoir characteristics of an entire new field, particularly since in recent years many new fields . . . are the result of stratigraphic rather than structural entrapment and lack surface expression and sharp structural definition.[3]

It is common for a large area over a structure to be already leased when a discovery is made. If leases are about to expire, they can be

[2] *Opportunity for Benefits Through Increased Use of Competitive Bidding to Award Oil and Gas Leases on Federal Lands,* Report to the Congress by the Comptroller General of the United States (Washington, D.C., General Accounting Office, 1970) p. 7.

[3] Ibid., pp. 8–9.

extended for two years and so long thereafter as oil or gas is produced in paying quantities by the commencement and diligent prosecution of drilling operations (see chapter 2, page 11). Thus, even allowing for the establishment of a known geological structure, the Department of the Interior may have little opportunity to lease lands competitively. The upshot is that in most cases lands that later turn out to be productive are acquired noncompetitively, and large windfalls of pure economic rent accrue to the original lessees or to their assigns. Such windfalls do not alter the margin of profitable exploration and development, and it would be better economically if they could be captured by the government and used to displace equivalent taxes.

This is not to say, of course, that the government gets no revenue from noncompetitive leasing. As noted above, a filing fee of $10 is required of each applicant for each lease unit, and this fee is not refunded. The result is a system similar to a lottery. For a very small investment, "any shoe clerk" (in the language of actual oil and gas operators) can acquire a chance to secure a lease of federal land. If he is lucky and his application is drawn first in the public drawing, he has a more or less valuable property which he can assign to an oil and gas operator for possible profit. (He must pay in advance an annual rental of 50 cents per acre while the lease is held.) If the lease turns out to cover a good prospect of oil or gas production, the profit may be very large indeed. If the applicant fails to win a lease, he has lost very little. Like any lottery with cheap tickets and large prizes, this one attracts numerous "players," most of whom have no connection with the oil and gas industry.[4] To facilitate large-scale participation by nonoperators, an industry of private leasing services has sprung up in the public land areas. These services advertise widely that for a fee they will act as agents in filing lease applications, and will finance advance rental deposits.[5] That such services flourish is evidence that large numbers of lease applicants are often attracted, each paying his $10 per application into the coffers of the government.[6]

---

[4] The BLM estimates that less than 5 percent of lease awardees ever engage in oil and gas development activity (ibid., p. 26).

[5] Ibid., p. 52.

[6] Ibid., pp. 18–19. The GAO study also mentions the sale of 408 noncompetitive leases in one county in Wyoming (1965–68) for which there were 41,403 applications.

But substantial application fees are no satisfactory justification for noncompetitive leasing. In the first place, the Department of the Interior has no way of knowing whether such fees in the aggregate amount to as much as could have been derived from competitive leasing bonuses. While fee receipts may be higher than possible bonuses on relatively poor prospects, the reverse is almost certainly true for relatively good prospects. The study referred to above (see footnote 2) found that the federal government secured substantially less revenue per acre than state governments that simultaneously leased competitively from lands in the general neighborhood of discoveries in Montana and New Mexico (1967–68), the difference being a factor of 20.[7] Evidence from resale values of noncompetitive federal leases in Wyoming (1965–68) suggests that the government received only a fraction (about one-fifth) of fair market value for lands in the neighborhood of discoveries.[8] In the second place, the lottery system of awarding leases significantly increases the resource costs of getting lands into the hands of oil and gas operators. Aside from the resource costs of the commercial leasing services, operators must negotiate with numerous lucky lessees, many of them residing long distances from the area of interest and activity. In interviews with this author, oil operators complained bitterly about the nuisance and expense associated with securing lease assignments from lessees who know nothing about the real prospects on their land but who are naturally intent on making the largest possible profit. With such a small initial investment and an annual rental of only 50 cents per acre, many hopeful lessees are in no hurry to sell their interests to active operators. Thus the system not only costs the government economic rent, transferring it haphazardly to lucky speculators, but it reduces the efficiency with which prospective mineral lands are allocated to productive users.

We conclude, accordingly, that federal mineral leases should be awarded only by competitive bidding, regardless of location with respect to known geological structures. Competitive lease sales would involve no more administrative cost than the present lottery system, probably would result in greater capture by the government of economic rent, and would improve the efficiency of resource allocation.

[7] Ibid., pp. 12–17.
[8] Ibid., pp. 18–19.

THE ORAL AUCTION VERSUS SEALED BIDS

In the awarding of mineral leases by competitive bidding in the United States the bidding may be by oral auction, sealed bids, or a combination of the two.[9] The Bureau of Land Management (BLM) of the Department of the Interior relies exclusively on sealed bids in mineral leasing, although regulations permit oral auctions in the case of onshore public lands (see chapter 2, pages 10 and 14), while a few states use oral auctions in oil and gas leasing.[10] The experience of these states, plus the experience of the Interior Department in marketing timber by the oral auction method, provides a basis on which to compare the two methods.

The essential characteristics of the oral auction are the necessary presence at the sale of persons authorized to make decisions on the spot, early establishment of the number and identity of competitors, the ability of bidders to react to competitive bids, the ability of bidders to give implicit signals to competitors, the possibility of punitive bidding, and the possible development of an emotional atmosphere in the bidding.

An auction may be opened by the establishment of a minimum acceptable price. If so, the first bidder may choose to bid only a token amount more, since he will be able to react to any other bids. If no other bids are made, he acquires the lease at close to the minimum acceptable price. If other bids are made, the number and identities of competitors are quickly established and the subsequent bidding may reflect what each bidder knows about the others—their resources, particular interests, characteristic bidding practices, and so forth. Under ideal circumstances bidders will be uncertain about the behavior of others, and each will continue bidding up the price until either a point is reached where the price is inconsistent with an acceptable rate of return to the bidder or all other bidders drop out. The resultant price thus tends to be above that considered to be just consistent with an acceptable rate of return to the next-to-last bidder, and equal to or

[9] The definitive discussion of this subject is Walter J. Mead, "Natural Resource Disposal Policy—Oral Auction Versus Sealed Bids," *Natural Resources Journal* vol. 7 (April 1967) pp. 194–225. The text discussion draws heavily upon it.
[10] Ibid., p. 198.

below the price that is so consistent to the last bidder. Where there is a high degree of certainty with which a lease may be evaluated, the reservation price, the price offered by the next-to-last bidder, and the winning price will differ little from each other. Where there is great uncertainty, as in the case of oil and gas leases on undrilled structures, these prices may differ markedly and the winner may acquire a lease at a price well below his maximum valuation: he need go only slightly above the valuation of the next-to-last bidder.

Under less than ideal circumstances bidders know each other well and can be guided in bidding strategy by what they know. A given bidder may signal to the others that he is determined to secure a particular lease by making what appears to be an unnecessarily high initial bid. If the others believe in such determination, they may let him have his lease without a fight. They may then expect reciprocation when "their" leases come up for sale and they give a similar signal. The result is lower prices (and higher rates of return) for all. Or a given bidder in strong financial circumstances may "punish" a weaker bidder for past competitive zeal by deliberately bidding away leases, even at unprofitable prices, that the latter has a special interest in. Such punishment may result in a lower degree of competition in subsequent bidding on other leases. Or bidders may recognize geographic areas of interest and abstain from serious competition for leases in others' respective areas.[11] All these circumstances result in lower-than-competitive prices, the degree of shortfall depending partly on the degree of uncertainty facing the seller and bidders as they attempt to evaluate the leases in question. Uncertainty reduces the ability of the seller to protect himself by setting a realistic reservation price and increases the possible gains to bidders of restraining competition.

The oral auction method also makes it easier for the leader(s) of an explicit conspiracy to police and enforce the agreement, since the leader(s) can observe any violation and respond to it on the spot. By the same token, however, oral bidding in the presence of the seller may

---

[11] The author is indebted to Wallace E. Tyner for the following comment: "(One possibility) is electronic 'oral' bidding. In this process firms would be isolated to prevent collusion and all bids would be entered electronically. The government could also enter the bidding when bids were below estimated 'fair market value.' Competing firms would know the amount of the high bid but not the identity of the bidder (unless it was their bid). This system eliminates some, but not all, drawbacks of the 'oral' auction."

make it easier for the latter to detect a pattern of noncompetitive behavior.

A significant advantage of the oral auction, where there are numerous tracts offered for lease in a given sale, is that losers on a given tract immediately know their status and are free to bid on tracts offered subsequently in the same sale. Bidders of limited capital may thus be able to bid on a larger number of tracts, increasing competition generally in the sale and enhancing the probability of such bidders securing at least some of the tracts. In contrast, where sealed bids on all tracts offered in a given sale must be submitted prior to the first opening, bidders of limited capital must select a few tracts to bid on, and if they fail to win, one or more of these are precluded from subsequently bidding on others in the same sale. The result is generally less competition in the sale and reduction in the number of awards to small firms. This defect of sealed-bid sales could be remedied, but at a cost of time and effort, by sequential bidding, which will be discussed in chapter 6.

Turning now more generally to the method of sealed bids, we can say that its essential characteristics are as follows: persons authorized to make major decisions are not required to attend the sale; the number and identities of competitors for a given tract are unknown to bidders at the time of bidding; the bidders are unable to react to competitive bids; and the bidders are unable to give implicit signals or to engage in punitive bidding. Sealed bidding is also likely to be more calculating and free of emotion than oral bidding.

In the typical sealed-bid sale, at least as practiced by the BLM, bidders do not know the reservation price of the seller. Thus they are not tempted to bid low simply because the seller places a low valuation on the tract in question. They also know that if they bid lower than a competitor on a tract, they will have no opportunity to respond with a still higher bid, and that the funds underlying an unsuccessful bid cannot be used to bid on some other tract in the sale. They do not know with certainty who their competitors for a given tract will be and thus cannot select with certainty a strategy adapted to the characteristics of such competitors. They cannot give implicit signals and establish a claim to a particular tract or group of tracts that competitors might respect. They cannot in the same sale punish other bidders by deliberately taking away from them tracts that they especially want. Under these circumstances, every bidder seriously wanting a tract is strongly motivated to make a bid which closely approximates the bidder's valuation of the tract.

If there were a high degree of certainty about the valuation of a tract, the results of sealed bidding need not be significantly different from those of an oral auction. In each case the winning bid would be equal to, or only slightly more than, the reservation price; and the reservation price would closely approximate true value to a competent competitive bidder. With uncertainty as to value, however, which is especially typical of oil and gas leasing, the results may be substantially different. In an oral auction, as we have seen, the reservation price may be well below some bidders' valuations, but the winning bidder may need to offer scarcely more; in any case, scarcely more than the second-highest bidder offers. But in a sealed-bid sale the winner tends to be the bidder with the highest valuation, which may be much in excess of either the reservation price or the second-highest bid.

Mead has noted the chagrin of high bidders in outer continental shelf oil and gas leasing at "leaving money on the table," that is, winning with a bid that is substantially higher than the second-highest bid.[12] The chagrin arises from the fact that the winning bid, seen in retrospect, was unnecessarily high; the winner has "wasted" money. But this is precisely what we would expect to happen with sealed-bid offerings under uncertainty, and in the absence of collusion. Each bidder tends to bid something close to his actual valuation of a lease, but the several valuations of interested firms tend to vary widely—hence a typically large gap exists between the highest and second-highest bid.

The foregoing analysis suggests strongly that under uncertainty, such as is characteristic of minerals leasing, sealed bidding tends to result in higher winning bids than does oral bidding. If we assume a natural bias toward underbidding in either system, due to uncertainty, then sealed bidding should result in the winning bids being closer to pure economic rent. We need not be concerned with a long-run tendency to overbid, for then realized rates of return adjusted for uncertainty would fall below the acceptable level, competitors would be repelled, and winning bids would tend to fall.[13]

---

[12] Mead, "Natural Resource Disposal Policy," p. 212. Mead's analysis of sealed-bid oil and gas leases by the BLM through 1963 revealed an average ratio of highest to second-highest bid of 1.91 to 1.

[13] However, in a study covering the years 1954–55, Mead and Krueger estimated that the internal rate of return on outer continental shelf oil and gas leases

With one qualification, accordingly, we conclude that under the circumstances of the mineral industries, particularly oil and gas, sealed bidding is more conducive to the capture of pure economic rent than is oral bidding. The qualification has to do with sequential bidding. As noted earlier, in oral bidding the losers on one tract are free to bid on any other tract in the same sale until financial resources are exhausted. But where sealed bids on all tracts up for lease must be in before any is opened, losers on the earlier tracts normally do not have an opportunity to use the freed funds to bid on other tracts. Small firms with limited capital may thus be able to bid only on a small number of tracts, and to win fewer leases in a given sale than they could finance. To the extent that this is true, competition in both the short and the long run is reduced. In chapter 6 we shall consider how the introduction of sequential bidding into a sealed-bid system might improve the latter.

THE RATE OF LEASING

How fast should federal lands be made available for lease? To the extent that promising lands are already under lease (notably potential oil and gas lands onshore), the rate of new leasing is limited by the rate of expiration or other termination of existing leases. But vast areas of the outer continental shelf and the public domain are yet to be leased for the production of oil and gas or of coal and oil shale, and the government has considerable freedom as to the rate at which these lands will be offered for lease in the future.[14] It is these unleased lands that we shall be concerned with.

In addressing the question of the rate of leasing we shall first discuss some general considerations and then take up the matter in relation to different minerals, each of which presents somewhat different problems.

---

in those years was only 7.5 percent *before taxes.* Even considering that the effective tax rate for oil and gas firms was well below the average for corporations, due to the percentage depletion allowance and expensing privileges, this rate of return is well below a "normal" one for the industry (at least 10 percent after taxes). See W. J. Mead and R. B. Krueger, *Studies of the Outer Continental Shelf Lands of the United States,* vol. 1, a report prepared for the Public Land Law Review Commission (Washington, D.C., PLLRC, 1968), p. 526.

[14] Coal leasing has been under a moratorium since 1971, but undoubtedly leasing will resume in the near future under the Federal Coal Leasing Amendments Act of 1976 (90 Stat. 1083–1092). Near future offers of oil shale leases are problematical, since it appears that lessees in the single 1974 sale are unable to proceed profitably with development and production.

GENERAL CONSIDERATIONS

Our assumed objective, in terms of which we evaluate the rate of leasing, is to capture a maximum of the present value of pure economic rent generated by the lands in question. Here we must give special emphasis to "present value," for the rate of leasing obviously affects the time at which rent will be captured. Accelerated leasing means, generally, that rent will be captured earlier; decelerated, later. Different streams of rent can only be evaluated and compared by discounting them to the present at the market real rate of interest, which in a world of perfect competition would be equal to the marginal social rate of time preference.[15] To government, as the agent in the land-leasing process for society as a whole, a unit of real rent now is worth more than a unit later.

It does not follow, of course, that because of time preference it is better for society to lease all lands immediately rather than over a period of time. Consider first the extreme (and unlikely) case in which the industry in question would be unable, due to nonland resource constraints, to explore and develop the lands in question at a faster rate. Faster leasing would simply mean that the typical tract would be held under lease longer before being explored and developed.[16] At the time of leasing the present value of expected net cash flow would be lower for the typical tract, and the rent offered would be correspondingly lower. If the industry and the government employed the same rate of discount, society would gain nothing from accelerated leasing. If because of less aversion to uncertainty the government employs a lower rate of discount than the industry,[17] then society would lose from accelerated leasing.

To illustrate this by means of a simplified example, assume that rent payments are in the form of a bonus, that the undiscounted rent (real-

[15] The marginal rate of time preference could be said to be 5 percent if at the margin consumers are indifferent to a unit of real consumption today and 1.05 units of real consumption a year from now. If the real market rate of interest differs from the marginal rate of time preference, consumers will borrow (or lend) and increase (or decrease) current consumption until the two rates are brought into equality.

[16] We assume here no constraint imposed by the primary term of leases.

[17] Government (society) probably does have less aversion to uncertainty because its survival would not be threatened, as a firm's would, by a run of bad luck.

ized at the end of each year) is $100 million for one tract developed in the first year and $100 million for a second tract developed in the second year, and that this development schedule remains the same, even though in our "slow" leasing case the tracts are leased in consecutive years and in our "fast" leasing case they are both leased at the beginning of the first year. First, assume that both the industry and the government employ a 10-percent discount rate. The result is as follows:

	Slow		*Fast*	
	Year 1	*Year 2*	*Year 1*	*Year 2*
Undiscounted rent (end of year)	100	100	100	100
Rent paid at the beginning of each year	90.9	90.9	173.5	—
Present value of rent at beginning of year 1	90.9	82.6	173.5	—
Total present value at beginning of year 1	173.5		173.5	

In the "slow" leasing case the lessor is paid $90.9 million at the beginning of each year ($100 million discounted one year at 10 percent). The two rental payments have a present value at the beginning of year 1 of $90.9 million and $82.6 million, respectively, a total of $173.5 million. In the "fast" leasing case the one rental payment is $173.5 million at the beginning of year 1 ($100 million in each of two years discounted at 10 percent). So it would be a matter of indifference to both lessor and lessee whether leasing were "slow" or "fast."

If the government employed a lower rate of discount (say 8 percent), it would prefer the "slow" leasing case, illustrated as follows:

	Slow		*Fast*	
	Year 1	*Year 2*	*Year 1*	*Year 2*
Undiscounted rent (end of year)	100	100	100	100
Rent paid at the beginning of each year	90.9	90.9	173.5	—
Present value to the government at the beginning of year 1	90.9	84.9	173.5	—
Total present value to the government at the beginning of year 1		175.1	173.5	

In the present "slow" leasing case the rent payments have a present value to the government of $175.1 million, in comparison with $173.5 million in the "fast" leasing case.

It is, of course, unrealistic to suppose that the rate of exploration and development would be unaffected by the rate of leasing. Once a lease bonus is paid, the rate of return to the lessee is increased by speeding up exploration and development. A short primary lease term also tends to induce an acceleration of exploration and development with accelerated leasing. In the extreme case (like the opposite extreme, unlikely) exploration and development would keep exact pace with leasing. In our example above, the fast-case undiscounted rent would be $200 million in year 1, which has a present value at the beginning of year 1 of $181.8 million (at 10 percent discount). This is larger than the present value to the government of the slow case at any positive rate of discount by the government. Thus the fast case would be preferred unambiguously.

But if we assume that exploration and development would be accelerated by accelerated leasing, we must take account of some other effects. First, acceleration of operations might raise short-run marginal costs above long-run marginal costs in both the extracting industries and their supply industries. Second, except where an effective floor under prices exists (more on this below), the prices of produced minerals would tend to fall with a faster growth of output, because of short-run inelasticities of demand. Third, due to imperfect equity capital markets and the necessity of small firms to rely heavily upon internally generated equity capital, such firms may be unable to generate equity capital at a rate corresponding to the rate of leasing, so that the competitiveness of bidding for leases is lessened. Fourth, the industry may be unable at first to perform desired preleasing exploration on all lands put up for lease, so that uncertainty is increased. Fifth, short primary lease terms may reduce the expected thoroughness of exploration, thus increasing uncertainty at the time of leasing. The effect of all these is to reduce the rents offered for given prospects; and the sharper the acceleration of leasing, the greater the depression of rents.[18] Consequently, we would have two opposing effects on the present value of rents: the accelerated receipt of rents, tending to raise their present

---

[18] One dimension of reduced rents would be rejection by lessees of some prospects that otherwise would be marginally attractive.

value; and the depression of undiscounted rents, tending to lower their present value. Which one of these effects would dominate would depend on how sharply leasing would accelerate and what rates of discount would be employed by the lessor and lessees. It is entirely possible that too sharp and sudden an increase in leasing would reduce the present value of rents; such an increase would, in any case, reduce realizéd undiscounted rents below the pure economic rent available, due to the elevation of short-run marginal costs above long-run marginal costs.

The effects we have described are largely short run (say, lasting up to five years) and are associated with a transition from a slower to a faster rate of leasing. However, there might well be a significant long-run effect: the reduction of competition in lease bidding. If for a significant period of time smaller firms are unable to generate internal capital at a rate corresponding to the rate of leasing, their share in mineral reserves will tend to fall and in the long run they will account for a reduced share of output (concentration ratios will increase). To the extent that increased concentration reduces competition, the latter will "permanently" suffer from what is otherwise a transition phenomenon.

We shall consider below an approach to leasing acceleration that may minimize adverse effects on rents and competition. First, let us note a relevant condition peculiar to oil and gas.

We indicated above that accelerated leasing would tend to lower output prices if there were no effective floor. There is over a considerable range of output such a floor in the case of oil and gas. The free price of oil is in effect set in the United States by the delivered import prices of OPEC oil. The domestic price cannot permanently rise above the OPEC price, for buyers are free to substitute imported oil for domestic oil. It cannot long fall below the OPEC price because buyers are free to substitute domestic for imported oil so long as imports are positive. The situation is illustrated in figure 5-1. DD is the domestic demand curve for oil. SS is the domestic long-run supply curve, assuming the present rate of leasing of federal lands. OP_i is the import price. OQ_d is produced domestically because it can be supplied at a cost (along SA) that is lower than the import price. Q_dQ_e is imported because the import price is lower than the domestic supply price of the equivalent oil (along AS). $S'S'$ is the domestic long-run supply curve at a higher rate of leasing of federal lands. The government can shift the domestic supply curve to the right (for a time) by accelerating leasing. If the curve is shifted to $S'S'$, imports fall to $Q_d'Q_e$, but the price remains at

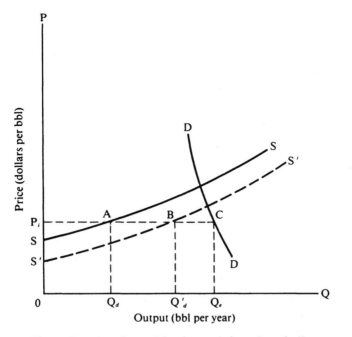

Figure 5-1. Accelerated leasing and the price of oil.

OP_i. Thus, unless the supply curve is shifted far enough to the right to intersect DD to the right of Q_e, accelerated leasing would not depress the price of oil.

The same diagram can be used to illustrate the gas market. Let OP_i now represent the regulated price of gas, this price being below the market-clearing price where SS intersects DD. Q_dQ_e now represents unsatisfied demand, partly met with imports (for example, liquefied natural gas) at or above the regulated price and partly met with substitutes (for example, coal) at a cost above the regulated price. Accelerated land leasing, by shifting the supply curve to $S'S'$, reduces unsatisfied demand without lowering the price, which remains at OP_i.

If shale oil extraction were commercially feasible at a price at or below OP_i (see figure 5-1), shale oil output would be reflected in SS and $S'S'$ and would reduce imports of conventional oil, for which it is a close substitute. Being a close substitute, its price also is in effect set by the oil import price. Accelerated leasing of oil shale lands would then shift SS to the right and reduce imports without depressing the price of oil.

Only in the case of coal, among the minerals we are considering, would the price be depressed by accelerated leasing of federal lands. Domestic coal demand is satisfied entirely by domestic production (and there are net exports), so a rightward shift in coal's supply curve would result in a lower intersection point (lower price) on the demand curve.[19]

Except for the price of coal, then, mineral fuel prices would be unaffected by accelerated leasing of federal lands,[20] and rents would not be depressed on that account. They would be depressed, however, for the other reasons given above (see pages 84–85); that is, the short-run rise in marginal costs, reduced competition by smaller firms, and increased uncertainty. Let us consider now an approach to accelerated leasing of outer continental shelf lands that would minimize these effects.

OUTER CONTINENTAL SHELF OIL AND GAS LEASING

There are relatively few factors to hamper accelerated leasing of oil and gas lands on the outer continental shelf. Except along the interface with state lands, where oil and gas reservoirs may overlap the border, all the lands involved are federal lands; there is no checkerboarding with state or private lands, as is frequently encountered in the onshore public domain. There is no serious problem of competing or multiple uses of the lands, since shipping and fishing are scarcely impaired, if at all, by oil and gas operations. The price of oil cannot be depressed by accelerated leasing; additional production simply displaces imports as the going world price set by OPEC. The situation is similar in the case of gas. Additional production simply reduces shortages at the regulated price. The only significant impediment is environmental considerations and resistance to leasing in new areas on these grounds. Subject to this restraint, the government has great freedom as to the rate of leasing.

There remains the problem of unduly depressing rents by accelerated leasing. However, as indicated earlier, the rent-depressing effect of ac-

---

[19] It may be of some interest to note that accelerated leasing of oil and gas lands, by reducing unsatisfied demand for gas, would reduce the demand for and price of coal.

[20] By the same token, except in the case of coal the federal government cannot raise the price of mineral fuels (and rents) by withholding lands from lease. Compare this with the discussion of monopoly on the lessor's side in chapter 3, pp. 41–43.

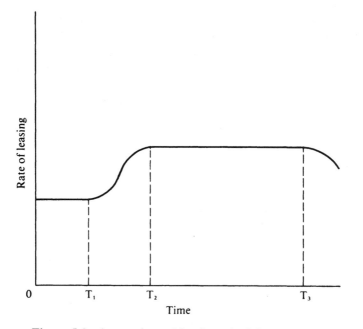

Figure 5-2. An accelerated leasing schedule.

celerated leasing is largely a transition problem associated with a sharp and perhaps unexpected (with certainty) change in the rate of leasing. If acceleration could be accomplished gradually and with a maximum of certainty, the rent-depressing effect might be very small and society might gain from the action.[21] Such an approach might have the following elements:

1. The selection of a schedule of leasing involving a gradual increase in the rate over, say, five years; a sustained higher (constant) rate of leasing for a long period of time, say, twenty years; and then a gradual decline in the rate as leasable lands are exhausted. Figure 5-2 illustrates such a schedule. Acceleration begins at time T_1. A new higher rate is sustained from T_2 to T_3, after which the rate declines again. The gradual increase in the rate of leasing would give time for the industries supplying drilling rigs, services, and materials to increase capacity and thus minimize the rise in short-run marginal

[21] The gain referred to here is the possible increase in the present value of pure economic rent, not necessarily the gain in security of supply of oil.

costs of lessees. It would give lessees time to accelerate predrilling exploration. It would allow production and cash flows to rise before the highest rate of leasing is experienced, thus helping small firms dependent on internally generated equity capital to remain competitive in lease bidding. The function of the long sustained rate of leasing is to create a situation in which the supply industries would be willing to increase capacity; they clearly would be averse to doing so if they regarded an acceleration of leasing as purely temporary.

2. The prepublication of such a schedule, indicating not only the amounts of land to be offered at different times but also the general geographical areas to be made available. The purposes here are to increase lessee certainty, to guide predrilling exploration, to allow productive lessees to make financial plans, and to assure supply industries of a justification for expanded capacity.

3. Relaxation of lease terms during and for a few years after the acceleration of leasing to a new high level. By giving lessees a longer time (say, eight years rather than five) to explore leases definitively, the lessor will recognize the problem of short-run bottlenecks in supply industries and enhance the value of lands to lessees.[22]

The degree of acceleration—that is, the difference between the old rate and the new sustained rate of leasing—should be a function of the total lands ultimately available for lease and the period of time over which a new rate of leasing must be sustained to assure an increase in the capacity of supply industries. Too great an acceleration would result in rapid exhaustion of leasable lands and enforced reduction in the rate of leasing in a short period of time, so that supply industries have reduced motivation to provide a permanent increase in capacity. Too small an acceleration would risk losing some of the benefit of transferring rent receipts from the future to the present.

The above recommendation depends in no particular way on an assumption about the future course of technological change. To the extent that technological change is anticipated, it will be reflected in the lease bonuses offered. Thus, ceteris paribus, if it is anticipated that future exploration or production costs will fall, lease bonuses offered in the present will rise. To the extent that technological change cannot be

---

[22] As Walter Mead has queried the author, Why not eliminate the lease term altogether? The interest cost of the lease bonus discourages speculative holding and encourages timely exploration and development.

anticipated, current lease bonuses will be unaffected, and the government runs some risk that it will capture less than the full economic rent eventually generated (if technological change is cost-reducing). Similarly, lessees run some risk that technological change, for example, development of alternative forms of energy, will reduce the realizable value of leases. These risks are inherent in a changing world and are no reason for the government to withhold lands from lease. Only if government officials are better at forecasting technological change than are prospective lessees should the rate of leasing be affected by the likelihood that technological change will occur during the lifetime of leases.

It should be noted that the Interior Department has in fact accelerated the leasing of outer continental shelf lands since 1973. Between 1964 and 1973 the average rate of leasing was about 0.5 million acres per year. In 1974 the rate was 1.8 million acres. It is now expected that leasing will average about 3 million acres per year in the period 1974–79, about 2 million acres per year, 1980–84, and about 1.5 million acres per year, 1985–89.[23] Thus, instead of a gradually increasing rate of leasing, the department has suddenly and sharply increased the rate, expecting it to peak before 1980 and thereafter decline. The time pattern of actual and expected leasing is poorly calculated, given the five-year primary lease term, to maximize the present value of pure economic rent. It is not surprising that the results of recent lease sales have been disappointing, as to both the proportion of offerings taken and the level of lease bonuses.[24] It is too early to analyze the effects of this time pattern of leasing on the competitiveness of bidding, but it is evident that thus far the capacity of the supply industries, particularly the rig industry, has not been a restraint.[25]

Of course, it is true that the major purpose of recently accelerated outer continental shelf leasing has been to reduce the nation's dependence on imported oil quickly, in the hope that by the time productive capacity ceases to grow, as it must when leasable lands approach exhaustion, technology will have yielded commercial substitute domestic sources of energy. The strategy may pay off in this sense. It is likely, however, that the strategy is already having a substantial cost in pure economic rent. An early return to self-sufficiency may not be consistent

[23] Federal Energy Administration, *National Energy Outlook, 1976* (Washington, D.C., GPO, 1976) p. 74.

[24] *Business Week* (April 28, 1976) pp. 72–73.

[25] *Business Week* (July 5, 1976) pp. 66–69.

with maximizing the present value of pure economic rent from federal lands.

COAL LEASING ON THE PUBLIC DOMAIN

Accelerated leasing of coal lands presents a number of problems not present in the case of outer continental shelf oil and gas lands. The federally owned lands are often checkerboarded with state or private lands; the willingness of potential lessees to bid for federal lands, and the size of their bids, may depend upon the ownership of or terms of securing extraction rights on adjacent nonfederal lands. This problem is intensified where the blocking up of an economical mining unit requires rights on both federal and adjacent nonfederal lands. The lands in question often have several alternative uses (for example, forestry, grazing, recreation), not all of which would fit into a multiple-use plan including coal mining. In many cases the federal government has only mineral rights, having disposed of the surface rights to private interests. Where it is necessary to use or alter the surface in extracting coal, especially in the case of strip mining, the necessity to acquire surface rights separately from, and in addition to, subsurface mineral rights may impede competitive bidding for the latter. Due to environmental restraints in coal use, transportation bottlenecks and fixed investments in oil- or gas-burning equipment, the short-run price elasticity of demand for coal is low. Consequently, accelerated leasing of coal lands accompanied by similarly accelerated mining might unduly depress coal prices and rents. On the other hand, accelerated leasing without some sort of incentive to increased output would serve no purpose except private speculation.[26] Finally, privately owned coal resources, in the East as well as the West, where federally owned resources are concentrated, are relatively more abundant than in the case of oil and gas. Federal restraint in leasing need not "starve" the economy for coal.

All these considerations argue against the approach to accelerated leasing that has been suggested for outer continental shelf oil and gas

---

[26] Note that a lease bonus, as contrasted with a royalty obligation, provides such an incentive, for it imposes an interest cost on delay of production. A short primary lease term also encourages early production, of course. Where early production is not prospectively profitable, however, accelerated offer of leases simply results in no bids or fewer bids or lower lease bonuses, or both.

lands. What is called for instead, we suggest, is a rate of lease offering that allows the coal-mining industry to secure rights to federal coal deposits when the latter are richer (that is, when they yield higher rents) than alternative state or private deposits, that entails no sacrifice of competition in the bidding for leases, and that reserves federal lands for the use or combination of uses that promises the greatest present value of economic rent. The first condition would tend to assure efficient development and use of the nation's total coal resources: utilization of deposits in the order of their rent-yielding capacity. The second condition tends to assure receipt of fair market value for coal lands, while the third tends to assure that all federal lands are allocated to their most valuable uses.

To make such an approach operational, we believe, the government should rely primarily upon nominations in selecting the lands for lease and choosing a rate of leasing. The more nominations for a particular tract, ceteris paribus, the more valuable the tract is likely to be and the more competitive the prospective bidding. The more nominations for federal lands in the aggregate, ceteris paribus, the more attractive such lands would seem to be relative to alternative state or private lands. A trend of increasing nominations in the aggregate would suggest undue restraint in leasing; while decreasing nominations would result in the reverse.

It is, of course, not necessary to offer for lease all lands nominated.[27] Considerations of competition may suggest that only those tracts receiving, say, three or more nominations should be offered for lease. Even if offered and bid upon, leases need not be granted where in the judgment of lessor officials bidding is not sufficiently competitive or the high bid falls substantially below the independently estimated fair market value.

A special problem exists where on adjacent nonfederal land an operator holds a lease and needs a federal lease to block up an economical mining unit. Such an operator would have an advantage in bidding for

---

[27] The Department of the Interior accepted nominations for coal leases in 1976. Some 971 tracts were nominated, covering 3,168,485 net acres. Tyner and co-workers estimate that strippable reserves underlying the nominated tracts are roughly three times the reserves required to support the estimated maximum coal demand through 1985. [Wallace E. Tyner, Robert J. Kalter, and John P. Wold, *Western Coal: Promise or Problem?* (Lexington, Mass., Lexington Books, in press).]

a federal lease since another federal lessee would have to negotiate with him to form an economic unit. Consequently, others may decline to nominate, and the operator in question may be able to secure a federal lease, if allowed, for less than fair market value. Compulsory unitization is no solution, since federal authorities lack jurisdiction over state and private lands for this purpose. To deny leases adjacent to nonfederal lands, on the other hand, would conflict in many instances with the aim of efficient resource use and maximization of economic rent. The only practical solution appears to be substantial investment by the government in independent determination of fair market value on such lands and the rejection of any bid that does not closely approximate it.

A similar problem, with a similar solution, arises where surface rights are privately owned and mineral rights are federally owned. Only the prospective lessee who held or could secure a surface lease would be interested in nominating the tract in question. Yet considerations other than the number of nominations and competition in bidding, such as richness of the coal deposit, may suggest early leasing of mineral rights on the land. Only if sufficiently armed with an independent estimate of fair market value could the government confidently lease the mineral rights to a single bidder.

Where a coal deposit underlies more than one tract of the maximum legal size and the deposit is most economically mined as a unit, then unitization of the several tracts may be made a condition of leasing. If transaction costs are not too high in the unitization process, such a requirement would enhance the value of any one tract and attract more nominations than would otherwise be forthcoming.

We have suggested that the rate of leasing may have a bearing on coal prices and rents. Too rapid leasing may unduly depress prices and conflict with the aim of maximizing economic rent. We hasten to explain that this does not mean to suggest that the government use a partial monopoly in coal lands to raise rents by withholding lands from lease. As was explained in chapter 3, the result would be antisocial and actually contrary to maximizing pure economic rent as we have defined it. Rather, our concern is that a sharp, unanticipated acceleration of leasing would, because of a *short-run* inelasticity of demand, depress realized rents below their long-run competitive level. In other words, we wish to avoid negative quasi rents as well as positive ones. For the long run, there is no good economic reason why the rate of leasing should not be such as to push coal prices downward, at least relatively, to oil and gas prices, and thus induce the substitution of a more abundant resource for less abundant ones. If nominations for coal leases are sufficiently numerous to assure competition in bidding, a long-run downward drift in coal prices need not be inconsistent with maximizing the present value of pure economic rent.

There is little danger of producing negative quasi rents in coal so long as primary lease terms remain set at twenty years. Even if leases are acquired as long-run speculations, the government need not receive less present value of pure economic rent than if it withheld the lands and speculated itself. There is more certainty about the presence and quality of coal deposits on given lands than in the case of oil and gas, and, therefore, less reason exists why the government's rate of discount should be less than that of private mine operators. With perfect certainty and the same rate of discount, the government has nothing to lose by leasing lands to operators who hold them idle for some years. Thus, we believe that the volume and trend in nominations is a reasonably satisfactory guide to the rate of leasing.

OIL SHALE LEASING

As with coal, we believe that the numbers and trend in nominations should guide the pace of future oil shale leasing. It is highly uncertain that the existing leases, resulting from the single 1974 sale, will lead to profitable production of shale oil in the near future (say, the coming decade). Given this uncertainty, it is doubtful that the government could secure as much present value of economic rent if new leases were offered "now," than it would by waiting until profitable production is demonstrated and the extractive industry shows renewed interest in the form of nominations. When given tracts receive a sufficient number of nominations to assure competition in bidding—say, in the order of three or four, given the government's ability to make an independent determination of a reservation price at fair market value—such tracts may be offered for lease without loss to the lessor. An upward trend in nominations, per tract and in the aggregate, may be taken as a signal to increase the rate of leasing. As with conventional oil, there is no danger of unduly decreasing the price of shale oil by too rapid leasing since, as a close substitute for conventional oil, shale oil's price is effectively set by OPEC and additional domestic output only displaces imports.

6

Alternative Bidding Systems

On the premise that all federal lands should be leased only by competitive bidding, we consider in this chapter several alternative systems or bases of bidding (for example, bonus bidding or royalty bidding).[1] The discussion pertains generally to all mineral fuels. In evaluating these alternative systems, the assumed objective is to maximize the extent to which the government captures the present value of the pure economic rent generated by the lands. This objective is the more likely to be achieved the more competitive the bidding (which, assuming independence of bids increases with number bidding), the lesser the degree of uncertainty or risk borne by the bidders, and the lesser the extent to which the bid variable affects the margin of development and recovery of resources. Operating efficiency and environmental protection, which are not particularly pertinent to the evaluation of bidding systems, will be discussed in chapters 7 and 8. We take as given the manner of taxing income from minerals production and assume that prospective lessees are generally risk-averse.

BONUS BIDDING

We shall first consider bonus bidding and, to emphasize its implications, assume that the specified royalty rate is zero or very low.

---

[1] In preparing to write this chapter the author benefited particularly from reading Robert J. Kalter, Wallace E. Tyner, and Daniel W. Hughes, *Alternative Energy Leasing Strategies and Schedules for the Outer Continental Shelf* (Ithaca, N.Y., Cornell University, 1975), especially chap. 3; and U.S. Department of the Interior, "An Analysis of Alternative Bidding Systems for OCS Oil and Gas Leases" (Washington, D.C., U.S. Department of the Interior, 1975).

As was mentioned earlier, the bonus is a lump-sum payment made at the time of leasing for the privilege of further exploring for minerals and, if an economical discovery is made, of developing and producing the mineral deposits found. Under competitive circumstances, it tends to be the present value of expected net cash flow beyond the point of leasing, where positive cash flows reflect sales revenues and negative cash flows include costs of postleasing exploration, development, production, royalties, and taxes; and where a normal, risk-adjusted rate of return on investment, including the bonus, is reflected in the discount rate employed. If a prospect appears to be particularly rich and cheap to exploit, the lease bonus tends to be relatively large. If appearances are the reverse, the lease bonus tends to be relatively small. The size of the bonus also tends to vary inversely with royalty and tax rates. In the extreme case of a zero-royalty rate the bonus tends to be maximized for any given prospect and, with allowance for uncertainty, to approximate all the economic rent available. Uncertainty creates dispersion of bonuses paid around (later) realized economic rent and, with aversion to uncertainty, depresses the typical bonus offered.[2]

The essential characteristics of bonus bidding are that it often gives rise to an often large front-end payment, that it (with zero royalty) settles the full burden of risk and uncertainty on the lessee, and that the bonus, once paid, becomes a sunk cost irrelevant to the exploration, development, production, and abandonment decisions (except that the immediate tax write-off of a bonus on surrendered leases tends to bias decisions in the direction of abandonment of marginal properties).[3] Only the last characteristic, which we shall consider now, is favorable to the objective of maximizing the capture of pure economic rent.

---

[2] The depression of bids by uncertainty aversion may be more than offset by the fact that winning bidders are the most optimistic bidders, not necessarily the most knowledgeable, and they may tend to overbid. Note again in this connection the study by W. J. Mead and R. B. Krueger, *Studies of the Outer Continental Shelf Lands of the United States,* vol. 1, a report prepared for the Public Land Law Review Commission (Washington, D.C., PLLRC, 1968), who found a low average rate of return to outer continental shelf oil and gas leases in 1954–55.

[3] This tax consideration may significantly qualify our general thesis that bonus bidding has the advantage of being neutral with respect to development decisions. However, it should be borne in mind that the net incentive to abandon is given by the difference between the present value of an immediate write-off of the bonus and the present value of amortization. This difference is limited by the fact that tax law allows amortization in proportion to production, which in oil and gas tends to be concentrated relatively in early years of reservoir life and thus has a present value not radically different from immediate write-off.

At each stage in the exploitation of a mineral deposit—leasing, exploration, development, and production—the operator to whom capital is not rationed decides to proceed if the present value of the expected net cash flow from the point of decision onward is equal to or greater than zero.[4] Outlays made prior to the point of decision are irrelevant. For example, except for the noted tax consideration, it does not matter what an operator has spent on a lease bonus and exploration if he is trying to decide whether to develop a discovery; he will maximize his gains, or minimize his losses, if he develops any discovery which promises to yield a net cash flow, including development outlays as negative flows, with a present value of zero or greater. Similarly, once production begins, the rational operator will continue production so long as the expected net cash flow has a present value of zero or more,[5] regardless of what prior development may have cost. Due to uncertainty at the time of leasing and at later decision points, he may retrospectively make either above- or below-normal profits on a given lease, but he will tend to maximize profits or minimize losses by behaving in the manner described.

Now, if the typical operator leases many tracts and on average correctly foresees cash flows, the typical lease bonus (with zero royalty) is a surplus of the present value of proceeds from the sale over the present value of labor and capital costs,[6] the payment of which surplus in no way affects exploration, development, and production decisions (except for the tax effect noted). It is just such a surplus that we have defined as economic rent. Thus, a competitively determined lease bonus tends to capture for the lessor all of the economic rent generated by the land in question. In this respect, then, the bonus-bidding system is ideal.

But it is less than ideal in respect to the other two characteristics: the front-end payment and the settling of maximum uncertainty on the lessee. The often large front-end payment would present no difficulty if capital markets were perfect and there were no uncertainty. Under these

---

[4] If the rate of discount is the just-acceptable rate of return, a present value of zero implies the prospect of earning the just-acceptable rate. In the decision to bid on a lease the maximum bonus offered tends, under competition, to be that which makes present value equal to zero, including the bonus as a negative cash flow.

[5] This assumes no net salvage value of producing equipment. If there is a positive net salvage value, abandonment occurs when the present value of expected cash flow from continued operations falls below net salvage value.

[6] Here we ignore taxes, which rarely represent the value of government services currently received by the specific activity being taxed.

circumstances, any honest and technically competent operator could secure in the market the necessary capital to pay a competitive bonus and carry through the exploitation of a given deposit. There would be numerous bidders on every deposit, and bonuses offered by the various bidders would differ little. Any tendency to underbid the true economic rent available and thus to realize above-normal profits for successful bidders would attract entries and drive up successful bids. Thus, with perfect capital markets and no uncertainty, the lease bonus would still be the ideal form of payment of economic rent.

But, of course, the facts are that capital markets are not perfect and that there is great uncertainty facing minerals producers at the point of leasing, the lessee's exposure to which is maximized by bonus bidding. Uncertainty means, among other things, that operators cannot finance the proving of deposits exclusively with borrowed funds, for example, from banks. A substantial proportion of equity capital is required and, given an imperfect equity capital market, small firms cannot raise such capital on equal terms with large firms. Small firms must depend more than large firms on retained earnings. Thus the often large front-end payment associated with bonus bidding is a barrier to entry and a restraint on competition in bidding. It tends to favor large firms, which may in time increasingly dominate bidding for leases as small firms progressively fail in or abstain from bidding on the better prospects, generate a smaller proportion of the industry's internal capital, and must fail or abstain even more, and so on. The problem, therefore, is not simply the present degree of competition in bidding for federal leases, but the long-run trend in competition if the lease bonus continues to figure largely in the rent payment.

At a later point we will consider some possible modifications of the lease-bonus system that might make it more acceptable. First, we will turn to the other type of bidding system currently authorized by law: royalty bidding.

ROYALTY BIDDING

In order to emphasize the implications of royalty bidding, we shall assume that the specified lease bonus is zero or very low.

A royalty, as earlier explained, is a share in the output of minerals or their value, payable if and as production occurs. No front-end payment is involved, and no payment is ever made if production does not occur. Whereas under bonus bidding the explorer for mineral deposits stands to lose both the bonus and exploration expense if no commercial deposit is found, under royalty bidding he stands to lose only the exploration expense. Under pure bonus bidding the operator need not share proceeds from production (gross receipts) with the lessor, whereas under royalty bidding he must. Thus the dispersion of possible outcomes on a given lease, which defines the degree of risk or uncertainty borne, is less in the case of royalty bidding than under bonus bidding.

The absence of a front-end payment and the reduction of uncertainty borne by the lessee mean that royalty bidding is more favorable to entry and to competition in bidding than is bonus bidding. Small firms have less of a problem of raising sufficient capital to grow with the industry in question, and they can participate effectively in more lease sales. Less uncertainty means that all firms will discount expected cash flows at lower rates and will tend, on this account, to bid a higher proportion of the pure economic rent actually generated by the minerals-bearing lands. (Less rent will be absorbed into a higher rate of return on investment.) Thus, in some important respects royalty bidding appears to be superior to bonus bidding.

The argument that royalty bidding increases the number of bidders (and presumably the competitiveness of bids) is borne out by the results of a controlled experiment conducted by the Department of the Interior in outer continental shelf sale Number 36 of oil and gas leases in October 1974.[7] A tract was selected at random on each of ten separate structures and offered for competitive bidding on the basis of royalty rates, with the bonus fixed at $25 per acre. The other tracts on the structures were offered on the basis of bonus bidding. Of the ten tracts so offered, eight received bids; and the average number of bids per tract was 7.1. Of the 287 tracts offered on the basis of bonus bidding, 149 received bids; and the average number of bids per tract was 2.2. Analysis of the differences leads to several conclusions at the 99 percent confidence level: (1) royalty-bid tracts received significantly more bids than bonus tracts; (2) royalty-bid tracts received significantly more bids than bonus tracts with comparable evaluations by the Geo-

[7] U.S. Department of the Interior, "An Analysis of the Royalty Bidding Experiment in OCS Sale No. 36" (Washington, D.C., U.S. Department of the Interior, 1975).

logical Survey; and (3) more new bidders were attracted to the royalty tracts than to the bonus tracts.[8]

However, the statistical significance of differences was not sufficiently high to support unequivocally the propositions that (1) royalty-bid tracts received significantly more bids than bonus tracts on the same structure; (2) new bidders are more likely to win on royalty tracts; (3) major oil companies (the top eight producers) comprise a smaller percentage of bidders on royalty tracts; and (4) major oil companies comprise a smaller percentage of the winners on royalty tracts. Thus, while royalty bidding seems to attract more bidders, it does not necessarily result in greater relative success of independent operators. The principal issue, however, is competitiveness of bidding, and that may be increased without implying greater relative success of any particular group of operators.

But what of the effect of royalty bidding on the margin of development and recovery of mineral deposits? It is at once apparent that the higher a royalty rate is, the more likely it will result in some discoveries not being developed and in the early abandonment of all. This is because a royalty represents a negative cash flow in the evaluation of expected proceeds from development and production. The higher the royalty rate, the lower is the present value of expected net cash flow, ceteris paribus; thus the fewer discoveries that can be economically developed, and the less complete the exhaustion of deposits when economical production can no longer be sustained.[9]

To put the matter in terms of the theory of rent that we discussed in chapter 3, it is necessary to study figure 3–7 (see page 37). In figure 3–7, the curve CC represents equilibrium points on a producing unit's long-run average cost curves, as these curves shift with depletion of a mineral deposit over time. The costs in question are labor and capital costs (that is, social costs), and the difference between CC and P_oA is rent per unit, where OP_o is the prevailing competitive price. From a social point of view, the appropriate abandonment time is T_n, where CC intersects P_oA. This would in fact be the abandonment time if rent were paid in the form of a lease bonus. But suppose instead a royalty

---

[8] *New bidders* are defined as those presently holding no interest in an outer continental shelf lease and not having bid since December 1973.

[9] Also, whereas bonus bidding is neutral with respect to capacity initially installed, royalty bidding tends to distort it downward. This is because a producer with a royalty to pay can transfer less cash flow from future to present by installing additional capacity.

of CE per unit is paid. Now abandonment is at T'_n, where EE intersects P_oA, and a substantial amount of the deposit goes unproduced that could be produced at a social cost (along DA) less than its value (along BA). The economic rent captured (proportionate to $CDBP_o$) is less than that generated by the land in question (proportionate to CP_oA). If the contractual royalty rate were CP_o, the mineral deposit represented here would not even be developed. Abandonment would occur immediately after discovery, and all the rent would be lost to society. Thus, on account of its effect on the margin of development and production, royalty bidding is inferior to bonus bidding.

In defense of royalty bidding it may be argued (1) that the Department of the Interior has the authority under existing law to reduce royalty rates that are too high to permit economical development and production of mineral deposits, and (2) that contractual rates established in royalty bidding are unlikely to be so high as to make early abandonment a problem. With regard to the first point, if the Department of the Interior were freely to adjust royalty rates that turned out to be too high, then the competitive system of establishing the winning bidder would tend to break down. As the department established a record of "appropriate" adjustments, prospective lessees would tend to bid higher and higher, regardless of their expected costs, and winners would not necessarily be the most efficient operators. After adjusting the royalty rate to accommodate the winner, the Department of the Interior could not be sure that it had received the maximum rent available. Nor could it be sure that the second or third highest bidder, with possibly lower costs, would not have generated more rent after royalty adjustment than the actual winner. Moreover, the department would have to systematically measure the costs of winning bidders, a costly task that would invite charges of favoritism.

With regard to the second point, the winning royalty bids in the experiment referred to above (outer continental shelf sale Number 36) were quite high. They ranged from a low of 51.8 percent to a high of 82.2 percent of the value of production. The bids by tract were consistent also with great bidder uncertainty. On the tract valued most highly by the Geological Survey the bids ranged from 0.5 percent to 82.2 percent.[10] Such uncertainty is likely to lead often to bids so high as to make ultimate discoveries uneconomical to develop without readjustment by the Interior Department.

---

[10] "An Analysis of the Royalty Bidding Experiment," app. B.

BONUS BIDDING WITH SUBSTANTIAL FIXED ROYALTY

We have seen that bonus bidding (with zero royalty) is superior to royalty bidding (with zero bonus) because of its effect on the margin of development and production, but it is inferior because of uncertainty and capital requirements. It is not clear what the overall balance is. It is possible that some combination, such as the present system of bonus bidding with a fixed royalty of 12½ or 16⅔ percent, would be superior to either extreme. The royalty component of the rent payment provides both the lessor and lessee some hedge against uncertainty, which tends to reduce the level of the effective CC curve seen in figure 3-8, and thus to restrict the contraction of the margin of exploitation; while the bonus component tends to capture the economic rent between EE and P_oA, in figure 3-7, without itself affecting the margin. Together, bonus and royalty may capture a larger proportion of pure economic rent generated than either alone. This possibility is illustrated in both figure 3-8 and the accompanying text of chapter 3 (pages 39–40); the argument, which is purely speculative, need not be repeated here. Since we cannot draw a definitive conclusion—cannot even suggest a practical experiment leading to a definite conclusion[11]—we must simply note the possibility and pass on to consideration of still other alternatives.

PROFIT-SHARE BIDDING

Again, for emphasis and comparability with the above, assume a zero or very low fixed bonus. For purposes of profit-share bidding, "profit" can be measured in various ways. We shall consider three. First, on the basis of taxable income, profit is gross revenue minus operating costs and capital consumption allowances.[12] Some share of profit so measured is bid, and the lessor's share is deductible for purposes of computing the lessee's income tax. Thus the total profit so measured is

[11] A useful experiment would necessitate trying several different royalty levels, each on a sizable sample of comparable leases, and would require perhaps twenty-five or thirty years—long enough to sample abandonments—to complete.

[12] Under current law and regulation in the United States certain exploration and development costs may be expensed currently; other capital outlays must be depreciated. For details, see Stephen L. McDonald, "Taxation System and Market Distortion," in Robert J. Kalter and William A. Vogely, eds., *Energy Supply and Government Policy* (Ithaca, N.Y., Cornell University Press, 1976) pp. 29–30.

divided into the lessor's share, income tax, and the lessee's residual net income after tax. Second, on the fixed-capital recovery plan, the lessor shares in gross revenue less operating costs, but only after the total capital investment multiplied by some factor greater than 1 has been recovered from operating profits. To the extent that operating profits allow, recovery of capital is accelerated, and the factor greater than 1 may be selected to assure some return on investment before the lessor begins to share in profits. Since a return to capital is built into the early recovery scheme, the lessor shares in a profit that more closely approximates the economist's pure profit, or the true economic rent generated by operations, than does taxable income. Third, under the annuity capital-recovery system, total capital outlays with accumulated interest are converted to an annuity with a specified interest rate and term, and the amount of the annual annuity is subtracted from each year's operating profits in order to determine the base of the profit share. Since the annuity implies a return on capital, the resulting profit base is a closer approximation of pure profit, or true economic rent, than is taxable income. Presumably, under both the fixed-capital recovery and the annuity plans, if applied to the United States, capital recovery for income tax purposes would follow IRS rules and the lessor's share would be tax deductible.

Profit-share bidding is similar in effect to royalty bidding. It involves no front-end payment, and it reduces the uncertainty borne by the lessee relative to the case of bonus bidding. In the same relative sense it encourages entry and competition, avoids discrimination against small firms, and decreases the rate of discount employed by operators. In these respects it tends to result in the full capture of the economic rent generated.

But also like royalty bidding, it may preclude the development of socially economical discoveries, and it may lead to premature abandonment of producing properties. This seems especially likely if the share system is based on the IRS definition of taxable income. Note that under the taxable-income system there is nothing to shelter a normal return on investment. It is entirely possible that on a leaner than expected discovery the present value of expected cash flow, with development expenses, profit share, and taxes as negative flows and all discounted at a just-acceptable rate of return, will be less than zero at the time of the development decision. It is also possible, then, that such a discovery, viable under bonus bidding, would go undeveloped and be abandoned if there were no negotiated downward adjustment of the profit share. Similarly, with a profit share as a negative cash flow, the present value of expected cash flow from the continued operation of a producing property would sooner fall below the net salvage value of producing equipment than it would under a pure bonus system (see footnote 9). However, these effects would not be as strong as those seen under royalty bidding since the dollar amount of the royalty per unit of output depends only on the price, while the dollar amount of a profit share per unit declines with rising operating costs. Thus, a profit share is rather like a royalty that diminishes in size as depletion progresses.

The development-inhibiting effects would not be as strong if the profit share were based on the fixed-capital recovery plan or the annuity capital-recovery plan. Under these plans a normal rate of return on investment is to some degree sheltered from encroachment by a profit share. To that extent, a profit share cannot preclude development of an otherwise viable discovery. To illustrate, consider the fixed-capital recovery plan under three circumstances and assume that the capital-recovery factor (greater than 1) results in a just-acceptable rate of return if investment times the factor is recovered from operating profits in five years. First, if an actual discovery promises to return investment times the factor in five years or less, then the expected rate of return on investment is equal to, or greater than, the just-acceptable rate of return, and development will occur, regardless of the share of operating profits promised to the lessor. Second, if an actual discovery promises never to allow recovery of investment times the factor, then the expected rate of return is less than the just-acceptable rate of return, and development will not occur. (Nor should it, for it would be socially uneconomical.) But this result is independent of the promised profit share since the latter is never expected to be paid. Third, if an actual discovery promises to allow recovery of investment times the factor in more than five years but during the expected producing life of the deposit, then the expected rate of return during the recovery period is less than the just-acceptable, and the profitability of development and production depends, in part, on expected operating profits and the profit share beyond the recovery period. A sufficiently high share in this case, which may well be typical, would inhibit development.

The annuity capital-recovery system would seem to lie, with respect to the development incentive, between the taxable income and fixed-capital recovery systems.

Although superior to bonus bidding in regard to front-end capital requirements and uncertainty bearing, and slightly superior to royalty bidding in regard to premature abandonment, profit sharing presents a major practical difficulty. It is necessary for the lessor to monitor the financial records of the lessee. Under pure bonus bidding no monitoring is required, and under royalty bidding only price and output records need be monitored. But under profit-share bidding all financial records are relevant to measurement and enforcement. Disputes may arise over the allocation of certain costs to particular leases, since profit shares will differ among leases. Disputes may arise over whether certain costs are allowable at all. Litigation may be common. In short, profit sharing would be substantially more difficult to administer than either the bonus or royalty system.

BONUS BIDDING WITH A SUBSTANTIAL FIXED-PROFIT SHARE

Conceivably, the system presently used in the United States might be modified by substituting a fixed profit share for a fixed royalty, with leases being awarded to the highest bonus bidder. Since a royalty and a profit share have similar implications for capital requirements, shifting uncertainty,[13] and the margin of development and production, our comments (on page 102) generally apply. We need only add that a profit-share plan would be somewhat superior to a royalty plan in regard to the margin of development and production, but inferior in regard to administrative feasibility.

WORK-COMMITMENT BIDDING

Under work-commitment bidding leases would be awarded to those bidding the largest dollar amount of commitment to do exploratory work, with the lease bonus or royalty rate specified in the lease terms. The underlying idea is that thorough exploration of federal lands would be encouraged. The difficulty is that waste might also be encouraged.

[13] As Robert Kalter has pointed out to the author, profit sharing results in the spreading of all risk whereas royalty sharing affects only reserve and price risk.

Under bonus bidding the lessee commits himself to explore up to the point where marginal cost equals the marginal value of information acquired. If there are no external benefits from exploration, this is the optimum amount of exploration. However, under work-commitment bidding uncertainty might, in many instances, lead prospective lessees to commit themselves to an amount of exploration expenditure that would turn out to be excessive, in that the expenditure would go beyond the point where marginal cost equals marginal benefit. Since the lessee would be obliged to pay to the government any amount of the commitment in excess of actual expenditures, the marginal expenditure would, in effect, be costless to the lessee, and exploration would be pushed beyond its socially optimal level. The alternative would be to police expenditures so carefully as to prevent wasteful expenditures, but this would be administratively difficult and would lead to dispute over matters of judgment under conditions of uncertainty. We therefore reject work-commitment bidding as an alternative to bonus bidding.

SOME VARIATIONS ON THE BONUS-BIDDING SYSTEM

Since the bonus-bidding system has much to recommend it, we shall examine the possible variations in it that might diminish its drawbacks.

JOINT BIDDING

Joint bidding is the practice of two or more potential lessees submitting a single, common bid for a given tract. Private arrangements among the parties determine how costs and revenues will be shared, how the tract will be operated, and so forth, if the bid wins a lease. Joint bidding is now allowable in outer continental shelf leasing for all but a handful of the largest oil and gas companies, and presently accounts for about 85 percent of all bids.[14]

From the point of view of reducing front-end capital requirements, spreading uncertainty and attracting entry by smaller operators, joint bidding has obvious advantages. It allows the smaller operator to tailor

---

[14] Robert M. Spann and Edward W. Erikson, "Entry, Risk Sharing and Competition in Joint Ventures for Offshore Petroleum Exploration," p. 2.

the size of his front-end commitment to his means. It allows him to spread uncertainty by bidding on a larger number of prospects. It allows him to share in the expert opinion of his partners. It allows a group to assemble sufficient capital in order to participate in the bidding for the most promising, hence most valuable, leases. But it also reduces the number of independent bids unless the number of operators moving into joint arrangements is offset by new bidders. Thus, in some circumstances, it may reduce effective competition for leases, despite allowing greater entry of smaller firms. From the point of view of the present study, entry and participation by firms of all sizes are desired because of their supposed effect on present and future competition in bidding.[15]

Spann and Erikson have recently tested several hypotheses relative to the competitive effects of joint bidding for outer continental shelf oil and gas leases over the period of 1954–73,[16] during which time joint bids rose from about 10 percent to about 85 percent of bids cast. They found that (1) the average number of bidders per tract increased substantially over the period; (2) shares of the larger companies in leases acquired varied widely from sale to sale, contraindicating collusion designed to fix market shares; (3) the percentage of winning bids in joint ventures involving nonmajor companies substantially exceeded that involving major companies; (4) the percentage of winning groups containing no majors increased significantly, while, over the same period, the percentage of winning groups containing only majors declined; and (5) there were few cases of nearly identical bids, and in no such case were groups involved containing major producers. The authors interpret these findings as supporting the view that joint bidding has increased, not decreased, competition. The findings are consistent with those of earlier studies using a different methodology.[17]

---

[15] It may be argued, of course, that out of fairness or some sort of political right small firms ought to have equal effective access to publicly owned resources. But it must be observed that to assure such access at the expense of competition is in effect to subsidize all firms involved. In any case, our concern here is with capturing economic rent, and it is enhanced competition which contributes to that.

[16] Spann and Erikson, "Entry, Risk Sharing and Competition."

[17] J. W. Markham, "The Competitive Effects of Joint Bidding by Oil Companies for Offshore Leases," in J. W. Markham and G. F. Papanek, eds., *Industrial Organization and Economic Development* (Boston, Houghton Mifflin, 1970) pp. 116–135; and W. J. Mead, "The Competitive Significance of Joint Ventures," *The Antitrust Bulletin* vol. 12 (Fall 1967) pp. 819–850.

Accordingly, we have reason to believe that joint bidding significantly reduces the disadvantages of bonus bidding.

SEQUENTIAL BIDDING

Under the present system of bidding for federal leases all bids are simultaneous. Each bidder picks out the tracts he wants to bid on, submits his sealed bids, and learns the final results when the bids are read. If he fails to be a winner on one or more leases he has bid on, he is not given an opportunity to use the money involved to bid on additional leases for which bids have not yet been opened. Therefore, the firm with limited capital is restrained from competing for more than a limited number of leases in a given sale.

Under sequential bidding, bids could be opened in the order of number of bids submitted (randomly where the number of bids was the same), and after each opening losers would be given an opportunity to submit bids on other tracts not yet leased before the next opening. The effect would be to increase the average number of bids per tract and to raise the level of the average winning bid.[18]

There would be disadvantages, of course. The process of awarding leases would be more cumbersome and time-consuming. It would be necessary for those attending lease sales to have the authority to make critical decisions on the spot, or else to come with complex contingency plans. Since different amounts would be bid on different leases, it might be difficult to accompany each bid with partial payment in the required form. These and possibly other disadvantages might well outweigh the benefits, but an experiment or two could settle the question. The proposal seems to be worth trying.

REDUCTION OF TRACT SIZE

Outer continental shelf lease tracts are ordinarily about 5,000 acres in size. Where prospects appear good, this size requires a very large

[18] Wallace Tyner suggests to the author that to prevent collusion in sequential bids officials might announce only the amount of the winning bid but not the identity of the winning bidder.

investment in a lease bonus in order to acquire access to what is usually a single geological structure. It is thus difficult for the smaller operator to spread his risk. Lease units of, say, 640 acres, typical of onshore oil and gas leasing, would facilitate participation of such operators and increase the competitiveness of bidding.

Aside from making sales more cumbersome and of longer duration, the difficulty with this proposal is that of forming economical units of operation. The more leaseholders on a structure the more time-consuming and difficult it is to form agreements on sharing a common drilling platform and to unitize a discovered reservoir for efficient operation and recovery. Leases of small size would be worth less per acre or per unit volume of prospective reservoir than leases of large size. As will be seen in chapter 7, the unitized operation of reservoirs is conducive to maximum valuation and capture of economic rent. Thus the advantage of an economical unit of operation, easily achievable with large leases, may more than offset the advantage of additional competition associated with small leases, particularly when joint bidding is available to smaller firms. This argument is possibly not as strong for onshore leases, where drilling is less expensive and a massive platform is not required.

CREDIT AGAINST BONUS FOR EXPLORATION AND DEVELOPMENT

Michel T. Halbouty, a well-known independent oil and gas operator, has made the following proposal, which has acquired his name.[19] A successful bonus bid would not be paid immediately to the government, but it would become an obligation of the lessee to spend that sum on exploration and development on the lease. If less is spent for these purposes, the lessee must pay the difference to the government. If the full amount is spent, then the lessee has no further obligation to the lessor except for royalties. In the latter case, which probably implies a discovery, the operator would, in effect, acquire a bonus-free lease. The advantages claimed are that it would encourage competition for leases, result in more thorough exploration and more discoveries, yield ultimately more revenue to the government, and save interest on delayed payment of the bonus.

[19] "Halbouty Concept Catching on as Independents See Benefits," *The TIPRO Reporter* (Winter 1973–74) pp. 16–17.

As with all something-for-nothing schemes, this one would not achieve its advertised results. Imagine a typical prospect that has a present value of expected cash flow of $10 million, composed of −$25 million for exploration and development and +$35 million for operating profits. Under present arrangements, prospective lessees would be willing to bid up to $10 million in the form of a lease bonus. But suppose the Halbouty plan were in operation, so that up to $25 million of exploration and development expense could be charged against the lease bonus bid. This would make the prospect seem more valuable—by precisely $25 million—and competitive prospective lessees would now be willing to bid up to $35 million in the form of lease bonus. The two situations may be compared as follows:

	Present value (in million $)			
	Lease bonus	*Exploration and development*	*Operating profits*	*Equal to*
Present situation	−10	−25	+35	0
Halbouty plan	(−35+25)	−25	+35	0

In both cases the lease bonus is the amount which makes the present value of net cash flow zero. Under present circumstances, a $10 million lease bonus is bid. Under the Halbouty plan, $35 million is bid, against which $25 million of exploration and development expense is credited, so that the net payment is $10 million. The two cases are economically equivalent, and none of the alleged advantages of the Halbouty plan are realized. The point is that competitive prospective lessees will bid away the net surplus, and the latter is unaffected by the financing scheme described. We might add that the same result would follow from the government's subsidizing operators on federal lands with tax money: the subsidy would be returned to the government in the form of higher bonuses.

The foregoing assumes that exploration and development outlays and operating profits would be unaffected by the Halbouty plan. But suppose a winning lessee, finding himself in the situation described above, would calculate that by spending $35 million on exploration and development he could increase the present value of operating profits to $37 million.[20] Under the present situation he would not spend the extra $10 million, for it would reduce the present value of his profits by $8 million. Under the Halbouty plan he would do so, because the extra expenditure costs him nothing; it is fully creditable against the $35 million lease bonus. Thus the operator would gain $2 million net by spending an extra $10 million. This possibility, known to competitive prospective lessees, would lead to higher bonuses bid, and so forth, until no further gain in the present value of operating profits on the typical lease could be had. Suppose the maximum of the latter is $40 million. Ultimately, then, the present and Halbouty situations would be as follows:

	Present value (in million $)			
	Lease bonus	Exploration and development	Operating profits	Equal to
Present situation	−10	−25	+35	0
Halbouty plan	(−40+40)	−40	+40	0

Under the Halbouty plan no net bonus is paid. All of the social surplus of $10 million has been exhausted into a net social cost of $10 million, the difference between the extra exploration and development expense ($15 million) and the gain in present value of operation profits ($5 million). Because of the inducements of the plan, society has spent an extra $15 million in labor and capital to gain an extra $5 million in oil and gas, a poor bargain. The plan would indeed encourage exploration and development, but would make society worse off. The results would be similar if exploration and development were subsidized directly.

Accordingly, we must reject the Halbouty plan as contrary to the objective of maximizing the capture of pure economic rent (or maximizing the value of mineral resources to society).

---

[20] Exploration aside, an operator of an oil or gas reservoir can drill additional development wells and speed up the rate of recovery of the resource, thus, up to a point, increasing the present value of operating profits.

INSTALLMENT BONUS PAYMENT WITH FORGIVENESS OPTION

Bonus bidding might remain the method of awarding leases, but with lessees being allowed to pay the bonus in installments and to surrender leases at any time and to be forgiven unpaid installments. For example, one-fifth of the bonus bid might be due at the beginning of each of the first five years of a lease, but if the lessee surrendered the lease at the end of two years, the remaining three-fifths of the bonus bid would be forgiven. Lessees retaining leases for five years or longer would pay the full bonus bid. Deferred bonus payments could bear interest if desired.

The direct effect of the plan would be to encourage early exploration of leases and to result in smaller bonuses being paid on leases that turned out to be unproductive. Relative to a full front-end bonus payment, however, it would perhaps result in less thorough exploration. This is because an increment to exploration would cost the operator not only exploration expense but additional bonus obligation as well if the life of the lease were extended.

The indirect effect of the plan would be to encourage competition and result in a greater capture of pure economic rent, given the number of discoveries made. It would reduce front-end payments unsupported by discovered minerals and make it easier for smaller firms to enter and compete. It would reduce the dispersion of possible financial outcomes on a lease and thus would reduce the rate of discount employed by prospective lessees. The discount-rate effect would increase the typical bonus actually paid, for on other accounts total bonus payments would remain constant.

To illustrate this last point, suppose that there is a fifty-fifty chance of discovery on any lease; that on a present-value basis exploration costs $50 million per lease, and a discovery is worth $200 million. Competitive lessees would bid up to $50 million in bonus for each lease. The situation is as follows:

	Lease 1	Lease 2	Total
Lease bonus	−50	−50	−100
Exploration	−50	−50	−100
Discovery	—	+200	+200
Net present value	−100	+100	0

Now suppose that on one lease two-fifths of the bonus is expected to be forgiven because of early establishment of unproductiveness. The two leases now have a net present value of $20 million. Prospective lessees would compete this away in the form of higher bonus on each unexplored lease. In the ultimate situation we would have:

	Lease 1	Lease 2	Total
Lease bonus	−37.5	−62.5	−100
Exploration	−50	−50	−100
Discovery	—	+200	+200
Net present value	−87.5	+87.5	0

The bonus bid is $62.5 million on each lease, but bonus paid on lease 1 is only $37.5 million. The total bonus paid is $100 million, as before. This assumes, of course, that the system does not reduce the discovery rate, which it might do, as noted above. On the other hand, the reduction of dispersion of possible financial outcomes would tend to raise the total bonus paid above $100 million by reducing the discount rate.

Because we have two opposing effects, neither of which is measurable ex ante, it is not possible to say here whether the installment bonus plan would be more or less favorable to the capture of economic rent than the present system. A suitable experiment would require a large sample of leases and an extended period of time.

WORKING-INTEREST BIDDING

At present, bids are made on specific areas of land, each one considered a separate unit for leasing purposes. One alternative that has not yet been discussed is bidding on undifferentiated interests in a large area overlying a geological structure, with the winners being those bidders offering the highest total bonus for the area in question. Each bidder would offer a bonus per acre on a specified amount of acreage (for example, 640 acres). Bids would be opened and arrayed in the order of the bonus offered per acre. The winners would be those, selected in order of bonus bid per acre, whose total acreage bid summed to the total acreage in the area. For example, suppose there are 10,000 acres over the structure in question and that the array of bids is as shown below. Note that only the first 2,500 acres are accepted for those amounts followed by an asterisk.

Bidder	Bonus per acre	Acres bid	Total bonus
1	100	4,000	400,000
2	90	1,000	90,000
3	80	2,000	160,000
4	80	500	40,000
5	70	3,000*	210,000*
6	60	1,000	60,000
7	50	2,000	100,000

The first four bids, and 2,500 acres of the fifth bid, would be accepted, since the total acreage bid sums to 10,000 acres, and the result is the highest possible total bonus for the area. (In the event of tie bids at the cutoff point, bids would be accepted in proportion to the acreage bid upon.)

Since the bidders receive rights to undifferentiated acreage in the total area, it is necessary for them to commit themselves in advance to participation in a cooperative plan of exploration and, in the event of a discovery, to development and production, sharing in costs and revenues on the basis of acreage shares. Other than the matter of shares, the plan could not be worked out, of course, until the winners were announced, and this would introduce an element of uncertainty in the bidding. Some winners might be difficult bargainers and delay the enterprise as a whole. Advance agreement to arbitrate differences might be essential.

It should be evident that this approach to leasing fits best with a regulatory regime under which unitization of oil and gas reservoirs is routinely required within a reasonable time following their discovery. The advantages and disadvantages of such regulation in relation to capturing economic rent will be discussed in chapter 7. The present point is understandable enough in the light of chapter 4; so it will not be discussed further here.

Working-interest bidding would alleviate in several ways the front-end capital and uncertainty problems of bonus bidding. It would allow smaller firms to tailor their investments in particular prospects to their financial means. It would allow them to spread risk by investing in a wider variety of prospects. It would allow them to spread risk on a particular structure by sharing in costs and revenues without respect to locational advantage or disadvantage. It would give smaller firms the advantage of sharing the knowledge and technical ability of others. In short, it would go far toward removing the disadvantages of bonus bidding.

As noted, however, it has the disadvantage of creating uncertainty regarding who one's partners will be and how difficult it will be to work out a cooperative plan of exploitation. This uncertainty would in itself tend to reduce bonus bids, an effect which must be weighed against the opposite effect of increasing competition and the spreading of risk or uncertainty. We are inclined to believe that experience with unitized oil and gas reservoirs is now sufficiently widespread and favorable to minimize the disadvantage noted.

INTERTRACT BIDDING

In intertract bidding,[21] proposed by the Department of the Interior for coal, the government would put up for simultaneous bidding a number of tracts but would not commit itself to granting leases on all of them. With simultaneous bidding on all the tracts, there would be competition among bidders for each tract, but also competition among high bidders since leases would not be granted on all tracts. To obtain a lease a bidder would not only have to outbid others interested in the same tract, but would have to bid high enough to assure that a tract on which he had bid would be selected for the granting of a lease. The supposition is that this situation would lead prospective lessees to bid more—that is, amounts closer to maximum valuation—than if winners had only to outbid other bidders for given tracts, with every tract leased to the highest bidder.

It is evident that the value of this system depends upon each bidder's knowledge about (1) the likely bids of others, and (2) the cutoff point in the granting of leases. With perfect knowledge on the part of everyone involved, the system would indeed result in a larger capture of economic rent. With total uncertainty, on the other hand, each bidder would be strongly motivated to bid his actual valuation on each tract regardless of intertract competition. However, a large bidder with bids on many tracts, although bidding conservatively, would be more likely

[21] This section relies heavily on Wallace E. Tyner, Robert J. Kalter, and John P. Wold, *Western Coal: Promise or Problem* (Lexington, Mass., Lexington Books, in press) pp. 94–99.

to secure one or more leases than would a small bidder whose bids are restricted to a few tracts. Thus large lessees may have an advantage, under intertract bidding, over small lessees.

Tyner and coauthors propose a modification of the system which does not depend upon good knowledge of others' valuations for favorable results.[22] Under their proposal, assuming that each firm knows only the value of the tract on which it has a comparative advantage and bids only on that tract, bidding would continue in "rounds" until there were no further changes in bids. Wherever the cutoff point, which would be known to bidders, every tract would be sold at just over the valuation of the highest-valued unsold tracts. We suggest that the system could be further improved by keeping secret, until the bidding ceased, the number of tracts to be let. Then every tract leased would go for just over the highest valuation of the next most valued tract. Thus suppose, to use the examples of Tyner and his coauthors, the following existed:

Tract	Highest valuation (in $)
A	135
B	160
C	110

If it were known that two tracts would be leased, both A and B would go for $110.01, just over the highest valuation of Tract C. But if it were not known whether one or two tracts would be let until the bidding ceased, and if two tracts were let, Tract B could be sold for $135.01 and Tract A for $110.01. Hence more economic rent would be captured.

It is unlikely that in the typical coal sale the bidders would have full knowledge of others' valuations, the condition in which intertract bidding would be most beneficial relative to an ordinary sale of leases. Moreover, as noted, intertract bidding may give an advantage to large firms. For these reasons, we are skeptical of the procedure, even with the improvement suggested by Tyner and his coauthors. We believe that in those situations where some bidders have comparative advantage, such as where a bidder already has a lease on an adjacent tract, the best assurance of receipt of fair market value is an independent, informed valuation by the government as lessor. Where government has such a

[22] Ibid., pp. 96–97.

valuation, negotiation may yield a higher percentage of economic rent than any conceivable bidding system.

SOME VARIATIONS ON A FIXED ROYALTY

We have seen that a fixed royalty has some disadvantages in regard to the margin of development and production. There are at least two ways of reducing the severity of the effect in question.

First is the *sliding-scale royalty,* according to which the size of the royalty is a positive function of the rate or value of minerals extraction per well or per unit area. Thus, for example, on oil leases the royalty rate might be 30 percent if daily production per well is more than 100 barrels, 25 percent if daily production per well is in the range of 76 to 100 barrels, and so forth, and to 5 percent if daily production per well is less than 11 barrels.[23] The basic advantage is that the royalty rate declines with declining capacity and rising production costs per unit, so that it is less likely to preclude development of a lean deposit or to induce premature abandonment.

Second is what we shall call the *tapered royalty,* which begins at a specified rate and declines each year by a specified amount or percentage, regardless of the rate of production. Thus the royalty rate might begin at 30 percent of oil production and decline at the rate of 5 percent per year until abandonment. (The annual sequence of royalty rates would thus be 0.30, 0.30 $\times$ 0.95, 0.30 $\times$ 0.95^2, 0.30 $\times$ 0.95^3, and so forth.) The logic of this system is related to the normal "decline rate" of the productive capacity of an oil reservoir. Like the sliding-scale system, it would tend to preclude early abandonment.

The basic difficulty with both systems is that they are not neutral with respect to development and the time-distribution of production. If the sliding scale is based on output per well per day, the developer-operator is induced to drill more wells and produce each at a lower rate. If it is based on unit area of land, he is induced to drill fewer wells per unit area and produce at a lower rate per acre. In the case of the tapered royalty, the developer-operator is induced to shift production toward the future and to drill wells over time in order to facilitate

---

[23] Present law does not allow a royalty rate lower than 12½ percent. Sliding-scale royalty rates are presently employed on certain exchange and renewal leases (onshore) public lands. (See chap. 2, fn. 62.)

that shift. As a kind of artificial cost, the royalty distorts decisions that ought to be based solely on real resource (labor and capital) costs; and these variations cause their own peculiar distortions.[24]

It should be said that the sliding-scale royalty is less likely to block development than the tapered royalty. The latter begins at a specified rate regardless of the basic productivity of the discovery, whereas the former automatically adjusts downward on the less productive discovery. However, a relatively low royalty rate may still preclude development of a very deep or otherwise expensive discovery. A factor in the formula inversely related to well depth would improve the sliding-scale royalty system. The formula could also be more generous for naturally high-cost areas (for example, offshore locations).

In any case, less distortion would result from a fixed but modest royalty rate, this to be administratively adjusted downward, as allowed by law, in the later stages of production. In such adjustment the regulatory authorities need be concerned only with operating costs, and it should be relatively easy to determine when an existing royalty rate would tend to cause premature abandonment.

SOME VARIATIONS ON A FIXED-PROFIT SHARE

Profit shares may also be established on a sliding-scale or tapered basis. The results would be similar to those discussed above (pages 117–118). However, the distortions in development and production decisions would not be so severe relative to a fixed-share regime, since profit shares in themselves tend to allow for differences in productivity and tend to be diminishing proportions of gross value of output as productivity declines with resource depletion. The primary objection to profit sharing, in whatever form, remains the problem of monitoring the financial records of lessees (see page 105).

CONTRACT EXPLORATION

The basic difficulty with the bonus-bidding system is the front-end capital requirement in association with uncertainty. If uncertainty could be reduced, the financial problem would be eased. This being so, why not transfer most of the burden of uncertainty to the government as

[24] Note that if a sliding-scale royalty were based on the *value* of output per well per day, the expected time pattern of prices would enter as a variable affecting the time distribution of production.

lessor, which may be assumed to have less aversion to uncertainty than the typical competitive lessee?[25] This could be done by allowing the government to contract with private operators to drill exploratory wells or otherwise definitively determine the presence or absence of commercial deposits. Leasing would then proceed in the productive areas on a bonus-bidding basis.

If the exploratory activity could be assumed to be as efficient and definitive as one carried out by lessees, the government, as lessor, would capture more pure economic rent. The reasons for this are that prospective lessees would save exploration expense, a saving that they would compete away in higher lease bonuses, so that the government fully recovers its outlays; bidding would be more competitive because of the easier financing and participation of small firms (financiers would face less uncertainty); and the reduction in bidder uncertainty would allow lower discount rates for evaluating productive properties.

However, there are several objections that may be raised. First, the government's "going into the business" of exploration would be considered inappropriate by many people and might have an adverse effect on business confidence. Second, since contract explorers (and the government) would not have the same profit motivation to do effective predrilling exploration, it is likely that the government's exploration program would be less efficient than private industry's. Third, not everything relevant to the evaluation of a mineral deposit is discovered in "exploration" (for example, exploratory wells). Development is really an extension of the exploratory process, defining limits, thickness, operating characteristics, and so forth; and extensive development may be required to reduce uncertainty substantially. Thus the government as lessor may be led to go deeper and deeper into the business involved, intensifying the first objection raised above.

These are significant objections, which suggest that the government, as lessor, might well sacrifice, rather than gain, economic rent by financing exploration for minerals on its lands.

CONCLUSIONS

There appears to be no accessible bidding system that has no drawbacks, or one that clearly and unambiguously is superior to all others.

---

[25] The government should have less aversion to uncertainty than competitive firms because its survival would not be threatened by a run of bad luck.

Of the two basic systems, bonus bidding tends to restrict competition and maximize bidder uncertainty, and royalty bidding (to which profit-share bidding is similar) has adverse effects on the margin of development and recovery. Therefore, we are led to seek combinations and variations that seem to minimize disadvantages. We think the following plan, while not ideal, is about the best that can be done:

I. Bonus bidding as the method of awarding leases
   A. Joint bidding allowed by all but the largest prospective lessees
   B. Experiments to determine effects of:
      1. Sequential bidding
      2. Installment bonus payment with forgiveness option
      3. Working-interest bidding
II. A modest fixed royalty of 12½ to 16⅔ percent, with administrative adjustment downward in later stages of recovery.

Bonus bidding allowing joint bidding, and perhaps installment payment, is neutral with respect to development and recovery and perhaps not excessively restrictive of competition. A modest fixed royalty reduces bidder uncertainty and increases competition while posing only a minor threat to efficient development, production, and abandonment.

We look with less favor on royalty bidding or profit-share bidding. The former is unduly harmful to efficient development and recovery, and the latter would be difficult to administer. We also consider contract exploration of questionable benefit. We reject completely the Halbouty plan of crediting exploration and development expense against lease bonus, since it would produce gross inefficiency in the exploitation of minerals.

7

Production Regulation (Conservation)

In chapter 4 we developed the theory of the optimum rate of extraction for a mineral deposit and suggested that unless prospective lessees could anticipate extraction at the optimum rate, the lessor would not capture all the pure economic rent available. It was indicated that in the production of minerals other than oil and gas profit-motivated behavior by competitive producers tends to assure the optimum rate of extraction; but in the case of oil and gas such behavior leads to an excessive investment in wells, too rapid an extraction of minerals, and too great a loss of ultimate recovery. Some form of regulation of the rate of oil and gas production is in the interest of society, not only from the point of view of conservation but also from the point of view of maximizing the capture of pure economic rent on publicly owned lands. In this chapter we will examine existing regulations pertaining to oil and gas production on federal lands and will suggest some changes with a view to maximizing the capture of pure economic rent.

ONSHORE PUBLIC LANDS

We must make a distinction between regulation of oil and gas production on onshore public lands and such regulation on the outer continental shelf. In the former area federal regulation is heavily conditioned by state regulation; indeed, the federal government, through the Geological Survey of the Department of the Interior, largely defers to the states in which federal lands are located as to the content (but not enforcement) of regulations. On the outer continental shelf, however, the federal government (through the Geological Survey) is the sole regulator, and since 1970 it has proceeded on a regulatory path independent of the contiguous states.

There are several reasons why the Geological Survey largely adopts and enforces state regulations of oil and gas production on the onshore public lands. In the first place, and most important, state and private lands are often interspersed among federal lands in oil- and gas-producing areas. It is not feasible to have two sets of quite different regulations applying to different operators in a common reservoir. In the second place, it appears to have been the judgment of Interior Department officials and, perhaps, the Congress that state regulations are generally appropriate and sufficient. In the third place, the federal government may have fallen into a posture of deference to the states because historically the latter seized the initiative and established primary jurisdiction on nonfederal lands in regulating oil and gas conservation.

The principal states containing federal lands on which oil and gas are produced are New Mexico, Colorado, Wyoming, Utah, and Montana. Except for New Mexico, these states have relatively mild oil and gas production regulations.[1] Their statutes and regulations define *waste* in physical terms (for example, loss of ultimate recovery of oil or flaring of gas) and prohibit such waste in oil and gas operations. The chief means of waste prevention are regulation of well spacing, compulsory pooling of land to form minimum-sized well-drilling units, regulation of the ratio of produced gas to produced oil in oil-and-gas reservoirs, prohibition of gas flaring, restriction of the rate of production from individual oil reservoirs when it is shown that loss of ultimate recovery would otherwise result, and encouragement of voluntary unitization of reservoirs.[2] New Mexico's basic statute defines waste to include the production of oil in excess of "reasonable market demand" on a state-

---

[1] New Mexico is a member of the group of major producing states, the others being Texas, Louisiana, Oklahoma, and Kansas, that have historically restricted output to statewide "market demand" and prorated allowable production among fields and wells. The other Rocky Mountain states have never based allowable production on market demand. For a detailed discussion of production regulation in all states, see Stephen L. McDonald, *Petroleum Conservation in the United States: An Economic Analysis* (Baltimore, Md., Johns Hopkins University Press for Resources for the Future, 1971), especially chap. 3, 7, and 9.

[2] Colorado has a statute under which a minority of interests may be compelled to enter a unitization agreement if a large majority (80 percent) voluntarily agree. See *Colo. Rev. Stat.* (1963) 1965 Supp., § 100-6-16.

wide basis.[3] In order to prevent such waste the regulatory commission each month estimates the market demand in each of two producing areas in the state (northwest and southeast) and allocates allowable output to individual wells on the basis of the depth and acreage drained. Since about 1970 market demand has been so large that the effective production constraint has usually been well capacity or reservoir maximum efficient rate (MER), where the latter has been determined. In any case, when market demand restrained allowable production, the wells on federal lands were affected, due to federal deference, the same as wells on state and private lands.

Federal regulations affecting onshore oil and gas operations are sufficiently general to be consistent with state regulations in the area of principal concern. The regulations give to the district oil and gas supervisor (under the Geological Survey) the authority "to require compliance with lease terms, with the regulations in this part, and all other applicable regulations, and with applicable law, to the end that all operations shall conform to the best practice and shall be conducted in such manner as to protect the deposits of the leased lands and result in the maximum ultimate recovery of oil, gas or other products with minimum waste."[4]

Waste is defined in physical or engineering terms:

Waste of oil and gas, in addition to its ordinary meaning, shall mean the physical waste of oil or gas, and waste, loss, or dissipation of reservoir energy existent in any deposit containing oil or gas and necessary or useful in obtaining the maximum recovery from such deposit.

   (1) Physical waste of oil or gas shall be deemed to include the loss or destruction of oil or gas after recovery thereof such as to prevent proper utilization and beneficial use thereof, and the loss of oil or gas prior to recovery thereof by isolation or entrapment, by migration, by premature release of natural gas from solution in oil, or in any other manner such as to render impracticable the recovery of such oil or gas.

   (2) Waste of reservoir energy shall be deemed to include the failure reasonably to maintain such energy by artificial means and also the dissipation of gas energy, hydrostatic energy, or other natural reservoir energy, at any time at a rate or in a manner which would constitute improvident use of the energy available

---

[3] *N.M. Stat. Ann.* (1953) § 65-3-3.
[4] 30 CFR 221.4.

or result in loss thereof without reasonably adequate recovery of oil.[5]

It should be clear from the foregoing definition of waste that federal regulations contemplate a rate of production from oil wells not in excess of the MER,[6] and that this rate is defined in physical terms and has no explicit economic content. In any case,

> The supervisor is authorized to fix the percentage of the potential capacity of any oil or gas well that may be utilized or the permissible production of any such well when, in his opinion, such action is necessary to protect the interests of the lessor, or to conform with proration rules established for the field. . . .
>
> The supervisor shall approve well-spacing and well-casing programs determined to be necessary for the proper development of the leases and assist and advise lessees in the planning and conduct of tests and equipments for the purpose of increasing the efficiency of operations.[7]

Thus, the supervisor may regulate well spacing and production rates, the latter to conform, if necessary, with proration rules that may be established for oil or gas fields. The term *proration rules* suggests market-demand prorationing but may also refer to well allocations based on a reservoir MER. Market demand as the basis of production is specifically mentioned elsewhere: "The production of oil and gas shall be restricted to such amount as can be put to beneficial use with adequate realization of values, and in order to avoid excessive production of either oil or gas, when required by the Secretary, shall be limited by the market demand for gas or by the market demand for oil."[8]

The flaring of gas is effectively prohibited. Thus, "the lessee is obligated to prevent the waste of oil or gas and to avoid physical waste of gas the lessee shall consume it beneficially or market it or return it to the productive formation. If waste of gas occurs the lessee shall pay the lessor the full value of all gas wasted. . . ."[9]

---

[5] 30 CFR 221.2(n).
[6] See chap. 4, p. 54. As employed by the typical state regulator, the MER may be defined as that rate of production from an oil or gas reservoir which, if exceeded, will result in significant loss of ultimate recovery.
[7] 30 CFR 221.10-11.
[8] 30 CFR 221.35.
[9] Ibid.

We have earlier noted that the relevant statute provides that lessees may enter into unitization agreements approved by the secretary of the interior, and that the secretary may prescribe a unit plan and require lessees to operate under it.[10] This provision for compulsion has never been used.

We see, then, that federal regulations governing onshore oil and gas production aim at preventing physical waste and are sufficiently broad and general to be consistent with a considerable range of state regulatory instruments: from control of well spacing to restriction of production to market demand, and from prohibition of gas flaring to encouragement of unitization. After briefly sketching the regulations governing oil and gas operations on the outer continental shelf, we will evaluate regulation based on the avoidance of physical waste.

THE OUTER CONTINENTAL SHELF

Outer continental shelf regulations place oil and gas operations under the direction of the district oil and gas supervisor.

> The supervisor is authorized and directed to act upon the requests, applications, and notices submitted under the regulations in this part and to require compliance with applicable laws, the lease terms, applicable regulations, and OCS orders to the end that all operations shall be conducted in a manner which will protect the natural resources of the Outer Continental Shelf and result in the maximum *economic* recovery of the mineral resources in a manner compatible with sound conservation practices.[11]
>
> The supervisor . . . shall inspect and regulate all operations and is authorized to issue OCS orders and other orders and rules necessary for him to effectively supervise operations and to prevent damage to, or waste of, any natural resource, or injury to life or property.[12]

Note the qualifier *economic,* in reference to the maximum recovery of resources. As we have seen, the word does not appear in onshore regulations. We shall see later how this word enters the working definition of MER on the outer continental shelf.

[10] 30 U.S.C. 226(j).
[11] 30 CFR 250.11. Emphasis added.
[12] 30 CFR 250.12.

Waste is defined in the regulations as:

(1) Physical waste as that term is generally understood in the oil and gas industry; (2) the inefficient, excessive, or improper use of, or the unnecessary dissipation of reservoir energy; (3) the locating, spacing, drilling, equipping, operating, or producing of any oil or gas well or wells in a manner which causes or tends to cause reduction in the quantity of oil or gas ultimately recoverable from a pool under prudent and proper operations or which causes or tends to cause unnecessary or excessive surface loss or destruction of oil or gas; (4) the inefficient storage of oil; and (5) the production of oil or gas in excess of transportation or marketing facilities or in excess of reasonable market demand.[13]

This definition is taken almost word for word from the corresponding definition in the "model statute" of the Interstate Oil Compact Commission.[14] It does not use the word *economic,* but in view of the earlier cited use of the terms in outer continental shelf regulations, the present words *prudent* and *proper* may perhaps be interpreted to imply an economic content in the definition of waste. There is no explicit reference to gas flaring in the outer continental shelf regulations, but the definition of waste to include "unnecessary or excessive surface loss or destruction of oil or gas" may be taken to mean that it is, in general, prohibited.

With reference to well-production rates and spacing,

The supervisor is authorized to specify the time and method for determining the potential capacity of any well and to fix, after appropriate notice, the permissible production of any such well that may be produced when such action is necessary to prevent waste or to conform with such proration rules, schedules, or procedures as may be established by the Secretary.[15]

The supervisor is authorized to approve well locations and well spacing programs necessary for proper development giving consideration to such factors as the location of drilling platforms, the geological and reservoir characteristics of the field, the number of wells that can be *economically* drilled, the protection of correlative rights, and minimizing

[13] 30 CFR 250.2.

[14] Interstate Oil Compact Commission, Legal Committee, *A Form for an Oil and Gas Conservation Statute* (Oklahoma City, IOCC, 1959) § 1.

[15] 30 CFR 250.16.

unreasonable interference with other uses of the Outer Continental Shelf area.[16]

Note the use of the term *economically* in reference to the choice of well spacing.

As under onshore regulations, unitization of reservoirs is encouraged. Thus, "section 5(a)(1) of the act authorized the Secretary in the interest of conservation to provide for unitization, pooling and drilling agreements. Such agreements may be initiated by lessees or where in the interest of conservation they are deemed necessary they may be required by the Director."[17]

The first example of compulsory unitization brought to completion occurred in 1976. Several others are incomplete and pending in mid-1978.

We see that outer continental shelf regulations cover essentially the same ground as onshore regulations, although the wording is significantly different in some sections. Of particular note is the injection of an economic content into what is considered appropriate with reference to ultimate recovery and well spacing. We shall shortly enlarge on this point.

OUTER CONTINENTAL SHELF ORDER NUMBER 11

Prior to December 5, 1970, the federal regulatory authorities on the outer continental shelf followed the prorationing procedures of the contiguous states. That is, off Louisiana, for instance, oil production for the area as a whole was restricted to market demand, and the total was allocated to fields and wells on the basis of well depth and the amount of acreage drained.[18] With the disappearance of spare producing capacity in the United States about 1970, President Nixon directed that after the date of effective regulations oil production from reservoirs on the outer continental shelf should not be restricted below the MER.[19] To implement this directive, Outer Continental Shelf Order Number 11

[16] 30 CFR 250.17. Emphasis added.

[17] Ibid. 250.50.

[18] For the depth-acreage schedules employed off Louisiana and Texas, see McDonald, *Petroleum Conservation*, pp. 154–156.

[19] 35 FR 18559.

was issued by the Geological Survey, with an effective date of May 1, 1974.

The order expands the above definition of waste to include "the failure to timely initiate enhanced recovery operations where such methods would result in an increased ultimate recovery of oil or gas under sound engineering and *economic* principles."[20] It directs that "the operator [of the reservoir] shall propose a maximum efficient rate (MER) for each producing reservoir based on sound engineering and *economic* principles. When approved at the proposed or other rate, such rate shall not be exceeded. . . ."[21]

The MER is, in turn, defined as "the maximum sustainable daily oil or gas withdrawal rate from a reservoir which will permit *economic* development and depletion of that reservoir without detriment to ultimate recovery."[22]

The question immediately arises, What does *economic* mean in the above quotations? The question is especially significant in view of the traditional emphasis on preventing *physical* waste and the almost universal definition of the MER by state regulatory authorities in purely physical or engineering terms.[23] At this time no final answer has been given by the Geological Survey,[24] although one statement by a (then) official of the Department of the Interior is perhaps indicative of current thinking.

[20] Geological Survey, Conservation Division, Gulf of Mexico Area, Outer Continental Shelf Order Number 11, p. 11-1. Emphasis added.

[21] Ibid., p. 11-3. Emphasis added. Temporary production in excess of the MER is permissible, but the excess must be balanced no later than the next subsequent quarter (Ibid., p. 11-7).

[22] Ibid., p. 11-2. Emphasis added.

[23] In conducting research for *Petroleum Conservation in the United States,* the author interviewed over a dozen state conservation officials and the staff of the Interstate Oil Compact Commission. All insisted upon a definition of the MER in purely physical terms, although when pressed several conceded that considerations of economic feasibility may occasionally enter.

[24] The matter is evidently under study. See John J. Schanz, Jr., *The Use of Maximum Efficient Rate (MER) as a Regulatory Tool,* a Report to the U.S. Department of the Interior (Reston, Va., U.S. Geological Survey, January 1976), reporting the results of a conference on the subject. Also see James W. McFarland, *A Selected Review of Maximum Efficient Rate (MER) and Related Resource Economics Literature,* Informal Report LA-6322-MS (Los Alamos, N.M., Los Alamos Scientific Laboratory of the University of California, July 1976). This author has had a useful correspondence on the subject with John Lohrenz, Conservation Division, Geological Survey, Lakewood, Colorado. He and the others cited are in no way responsible for this author's interpretation.

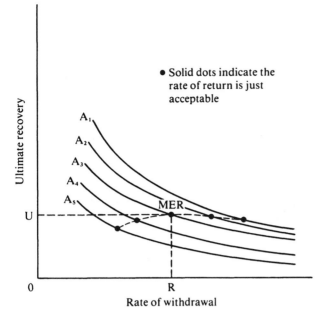

Figure 7-1. Determination of the maximum efficient rate (MER). Solid dots indicate the points at which the economic rate of return is just acceptable.

Jack W. Carlson has offered a diagram (figure 7-1) in reference to Outer Continental Shelf Order Number 11,[25] which we interpret to imply a definition of the MER as the rate of extraction from a reservoir which, chosen in association with the number of wells, results in the maximum ultimate recovery consistent with a just-acceptable rate of return to the operator(s). Each curve in the diagram (A_1, A_2, and so forth) represents the inverse relationship between ultimate recovery and the withdrawal rate, given the number of wells (hence spacing interval) in the reservoir.[26] The increasing number of wells is indicated by higher and higher curves, with A_1 representing the largest number of wells.

[25] Statement of Jack W. Carlson, assistant secretary, Energy and Minerals, Department of the Interior, before the Senate Subcommittee on Antitrust and Monopoly, Committee on the Judiciary, September 23, 1975, p. 20 (Mimeographed).

[26] The diagram, which is assumed to be illustrative only, tends to exaggerate the sensitivity of ultimate recovery to the rate of withdrawal and number of wells. To be more realistic, the curves should be much farther from the origin.

The family of curves, read from left to right, may be interpreted as indicating that the rate of withdrawal consistent with a given ultimate recovery increases with the number of wells. The broken curved line connecting the solid dots traces combinations of ultimate recovery and rate of withdrawal that yield a rate of return just acceptable to operators. The curve rises, as we read from left to right, because the positive effect of wells on ultimate recovery more than offsets the negative effect of rate of withdrawal, holding the rate of return constant; then it declines because of the reverse effect. The highest point on the curve, *MER*, represents the combination of wells and rate of withdrawal which maximizes the ultimate recovery consistent with a just-acceptable rate of return. Such a definition continues to emphasize maximizing ultimate recovery but inserts the condition that operators make an acceptable rate of return on investment.

This is one possible way of giving economic content to the definition of the MER. There are undoubtedly others. One such alternative is the optimum rate of withdrawal; but first let us evaluate the current systems of production regulation as they affect the capture of economic rent by the lessor.

THE AVOIDANCE OF PHYSICAL WASTE AND THE CAPTURE OF ECONOMIC RENT

The capture of pure economic rent tends to be maximized when, among other things, the expected value of a mineral deposit is maximized. Lessees estimate expected value in the light of regulations with which they must comply. If these regulations promise to limit expected value, then they have the effect of lowering rents offered below those potentially available. Regulations inconsistent with maximizing value are inconsistent with full capture of pure economic rent. Such regulations tend to absorb economic rent into higher costs of development and extraction.

To illustrate the effect of regulation per se, assume an oil and gas reservoir that is operated by a single lessee. This assumption is made to remove the uneconomic effects of unrestrained competitive extraction: excessive well density, too rapid production, and too great a loss of ultimate recovery (see chapter 4, pages 58–59). Upon discovery, the operator seeks to maximize V_0, as shown in Equation 7-1:

$$V_0 = -I_0 + \frac{(R - C)_1}{(1 + r)^1} + \frac{(R - C)_2}{(1 + r)^2} + \ldots + \frac{(R - C)_n}{(1 + r)^n} \qquad (7\text{-}1)$$

where V_0 = present value at time zero
I_0 = development investment at time zero
R = cash revenue in indicated periods
C = cash costs in indicated periods
r = rate of discount
n = expected year of abandonment

(For simplicity it is assumed that all development investment occurs at time zero and that net revenues are received at the end of each year.) The result is a certain producing capacity and a related planned time-distribution of extraction. Let us suppose that the production plan would involve no loss of ultimate recovery and would cause no physical waste. It and the well density would be fully consistent with current onshore regulation of operations on federal lands.

But now suppose the operator calculates that by drilling some additional wells he can speed up recovery, shift the receipt of net revenues toward the present, and after making an allowance for some loss of ultimate recovery, he can increase the present value of the reservoir. If he were free of regulation, he would drill the additional wells and accordingly change the time-distribution of extraction, because it would make him better off: he would earn more than the required rate of return (his rate of discount) on the incremental investment. It would also make society better off because, under our assumption of a single operator, the operator's relevant costs and benefits would coincide with society's.[27]

But the new plan of extraction involves some loss of ultimate recovery—some physical waste. Presumably, then, the regulatory authorities would not permit him to speed up the rate of extraction. In order to maximize ultimate recovery the authorities would require the operator

[27] Here we assume reasonably competitive markets and the absence of environmental externalities. We also assume that the operator can as correctly forecast costs and benefits as society.

(and society) to forgo a gain in wealth. They would require him to behave as if oil were the only resource worth economizing—as if the marginal rate of time preference were zero.

Now, if an operator as potential lessee knows that he will be subjected to this kind of regulation, he will be willing to bid less on a given prospect, ceteris paribus, than he would be willing to bid if he knows he would be permitted to exhaust every opportunity to increase the value of his property. He would bid less than the pure economic rent available, since the latter, by our definition, implies development and operation that is economically efficient—that maximizes the value of the resource in question. Thus, maximizing the capture of pure economic rent requires allowing operators to expect freedom to maximize the value of their property, insofar as their costs and benefits coincide with society's. It is only where private and social costs and benefits do not coincide that regulation is called for.

The foregoing suggests that what we should aim for is not the MER of oil recovery, as defined in physical terms, but the *optimum rate,* as defined in economic terms. The optimum rate of extraction (and optimum well density) occurs when the operator has sped up production to the point where the incremental increase in value is zero, so that on the *incremental* investment his rate of return is just acceptable.

It should be noted that the optimum rate of extraction is not fixed once and for all in a given reservoir. It fluctuates with changing expectations about prices and costs. For instance, a rise in expected future prices relative to present ones lowers the optimum (current) rate of extraction, for gain in present value is to be had by shifting recovery from the present to the future. The reverse is true when present prices rise relative to those expected in the future. The operator who knows he will be permitted to respond to changing expectations will be willing to bid more for a lease than an operator who knows that he will not be so permitted. Thus the use of the MER, defined in physical terms, as both a minimum and a maximum rate of production is to reduce, ceteris paribus, the capture of pure economic rent.

Let us consider one other example involving the physical waste concept. Suppose that our operator has a dissolved gas-drive oil reservoir, so that gas is necessarily produced with oil, and that the volume of gas is not sufficient to warrant a pipeline connection. The commercial value of the gas is zero. Under present onshore regulations he would be required to consume the gas beneficially on the lease or return it to the reservoir. He would not be permitted to flare it. But suppose the value of the gas is negative after allowance for the investment required to use it on the lease or return it to the reservoir. The operator (and society) would be made worse off by the prevention of physical waste in the form of flaring. The potential lessee who expected to be compelled to prevent physical waste of gas, regardless of the economics of alternatives, would bid less for a given lease, ceteris paribus, than he would be willing to bid if he were permitted to make the most valuable disposition of the gas. Maximizing the capture of pure economic rent calls for allowing the latter kind of expectation.

Thus the prevention of physical waste, rigorously pursued, may often lead to reduced capture of pure economic rent, and a reduced value of the resource in question to society.

THE OUTER CONTINENTAL SHELF DEFINITION OF MER AND THE CAPTURE OF ECONOMIC RENT

We have seen that outer continental shelf regulations frequently contain the word *economic* as a modifier of terms otherwise implying the prevention of physical waste. Does this remove the objection to physical waste avoidance, as discussed on page 131? Not necessarily. Consider the definition of the MER in figure 7-1.

Suppose that our lone operator of an oil reservoir initially develops the reservoir and extracts oil at a rate that both results in no loss of ultimate recovery and yields the operator a just-acceptable rate of return on the operation as a whole. And suppose, as before, the operator calculates that by adding wells and speeding up extraction and by accepting some loss of ultimate recovery, a rate of return on the *incremental* investment could be made above the just-acceptable level; that is, something could be added to the present value of the reservoir. Under the definition of the MER suggested by Carlson, the operator would not be permitted to make the change in production rate, for the reason that by refraining he increases ultimate recovery and still makes an acceptable rate of return on the overall investment. Thus, again, pursuit of maximum ultimate recovery results in loss of value to the operator (and society). Operators who anticipate such a constraint on their value-maximizing behavior would be willing to bid less for oil and gas leases than if they could expect freedom of action—less than the pure economic rent actually available.

On the other hand, we can imagine a case in which the MER (as defined by Carlson) would be reasonably consistent with maximizing value. Suppose our operator initially develops a reservoir to produce at a rate which maximizes ultimate recovery, but he finds that producing at such a rate results in a return on investment that is less than the just-acceptable rate. Suppose that he calculates that by drilling additional wells and speeding up extraction he could make on the incremental investment a rate of return above the just-acceptable level, although reducing ultimate recovery. Presumably, the operator would be permitted to make the change, for although some loss of ultimate recovery results, the operator would come closer to making an acceptable rate of return on the operation as a whole. Presumably, too, an operator would be permitted to flare gas if it would tend to raise an unacceptable rate of return toward the just-acceptable level.

Thus the Carlson definition of the MER, while not ideal, is distinctly superior to the traditional (onshore) definition, at least in terms of maximizing ultimate recovery without regard to economics. It comes closer to being consistent with maximizing the capture of pure economic rent. Nonetheless, we must emphasize that the latter aim is better served by pursuing the *optimum rate* (and associated well density), defined as the rate which maximizes present value; or by defining the MER equivalently. By such a definition, development and the speeding up of extraction would be allowed to proceed to the point where the rate of return on the incremental investment is just acceptable.[28] At this point, value is maximized; and operators anticipating freedom to maximize value would tend to bid amounts for leases more closely approaching the pure economic rent available.

THE ALTERNATIVE OF UNITIZATION WITH FREEDOM

In the preceding evaluation of physical waste prevention, with or without the condition of a just-acceptable rate of return, we have as-

---

[28] The Carlson definition errs precisely in making the condition of a just-acceptable rate of return apply to the operation as a whole rather than to the incremental investment.

sumed a single operator of the affected reservoir so as to remove the discrepancy between private and social costs and benefits that arises when reservoirs are developed and operated by two or more competitive lessees (see footnote 27). Recall that competitive operators, in pursuing their private interests, are induced to drill wells too densely and to produce at too high an initial rate because in their calculations they include revenues to be gained at the expense of neighbors in the same reservoir (see chapter 4, pages 58–59). We must say here that in all probability regulation to prevent physical waste, especially if modified to allow for an acceptable rate of return, is more in the interest of society—more conducive to capturing pure economic rent—than allowing competitive operators in a common reservoir freedom of action.

But we are not confined to the two alternatives of regulation to prevent physical waste versus complete freedom for competitive operators. A third alternative is unitization of oil and gas reservoirs, either voluntary or compulsory. What unitization basically does is to remove the possibility of gaining revenues at the expense of neighbors, so that the calculations of the operators as a whole (through a unit manager) correspond to those a single operator would make (see chapter 4, pages 62–63). With reasonably competitive markets and internalization of environmental externalities, the collective interests of the operators of a unitized reservoir tend to coincide with those of society. The operators fully bear the burden of the value of resources "wasted" (for example, reduced oil recovery or flared gas), and they can rationally compare this value with the cost of avoidance. In seeking to maximize the value of their property they also promote the maximization of the resource value to society. Believing that they will have full freedom to maximize value, they will individually or collectively (in joint bidding) bid for leases in amounts approaching the pure economic rent available. With unitization, the aim of maximizing the capture of pure economic rent can be furthered without any form of regulation specifically designed to prevent waste and promote conservation.

More specifically, first, unitization tends to lead to the voluntary adoption of the optimum rate of production (and associated optimum well density). The operators would push development and speed up production to the point where the increment to present value was zero (or where the rate of return on the incremental investment was just acceptable). With private costs and benefits coinciding with social costs and benefits such behavior would optimize the well density and production rate from society's point of view and thus maximize the available pure economic rent. If anticipated, this rent would tend to be bid away to the lessor.

Second, unitization allows the affected operators to adjust the rate of production—more exactly, the time-distribution of production—so as to search continuously for maximum present value as events unfold and expected versus present prices and costs change. Without the cooperation of his neighbors, an individual operator could not afford to adjust downward the current rate of production in the expectation of higher prices in the future, since purely individual action would entail loss of revenues to neighbors. Nor does the MER-based regulation allow operators to adjust production rates to maximize the present value under all conditions. Thus the expectation of unitized operations, by enhancing expected value under changing conditions, leads to higher bids for leases and a closer approximation to all the pure economic rent available.

Third, unitization leads to a more rational calculation regarding the disposition of gas produced with oil. Rarely does it pay an individual operator to return produced gas to the reservoir for pressure maintenance, for the expenses are his and the benefits accrue to all operators in the common reservoir. But with unitization both expenses and benefits are shared by prearranged formula, and the group of operators can compare the common benefits with the common costs in making a disposition decision. Thus unitized operators can make a value-maximizing choice among the sale of gas currently, the return of gas currently to the reservoir, or the flaring of gas. No specific regulation is required to protect society. And, again, if freedom to make value-maximizing decisions is anticipated, bids for leases will more closely approximate the pure economic rent available.

Fourth, unitization makes possible a more rational use of cap gas in an oil reservoir. As indicated earlier (see chapter 4, page 61), with many competitive operators in such a reservoir the protection of correlative rights may require cap gas to be produced concurrently with oil, even though it may be more valuable to the group (and society) if retained in the reservoir to facilitate efficient oil recovery. With unitization, however, correlative rights are directly protected by the sharing formula, and a choice can be made to produce currently or to retain cap gas on the basis of which option more greatly enhances the value of the reservoir. If operators could always anticipate being able to make this choice on an economic basis, they would tend to bid more for leases than otherwise, and the lessor would more fully capture pure economic rent.

Economically, unitization appears to be the ideal solution both to the problem of oil and gas conservation and to the problem of maximizing the capture of pure economic rent. It would appear to be in the interest of operators as well. Why, then, is it not voluntarily adopted in all reservoirs? There are several reasons, perhaps the principal one being that individual operators, often finding themselves with a structural or other advantage in a reservoir,[29] would lose net revenues if shares were equitable and acceptable to other operators. Other reasons include ignorance, mistrust of other operators, differences in cash-flow needs (for example, to service debt), fear of domination by larger competitors, desire to use one's own work crews (rather than those of a unit manager), fear of increased trouble and expense in management, and profitable obstructionism. Some of these reasons can be overcome with persuasion, but others are sometimes insurmountable barriers to voluntary unitization. Although many voluntary units are formed, most producing states have found it in the interest of conservation and rational operation of oil or gas reservoirs to apply a degree of compulsion to reluctant minorities when a large majority of operators in a common reservoir have reached agreement on a unit plan.[30] Federal law and regulations, as we have seen, provide for compulsion at the discretion of the director of the Geological Survey, without any necessity for majority approval.

As suggested above, it is this author's opinion that all reservoirs should be unitized, preferably before development is completed, and that in unitized reservoirs the operators should be given freedom as to well density, production rate, and use of gas. Specific regulation is required only to internalize environmental externalities once a unit plan is put into operation. The reasons for this opinion have been given.

---

[29] An operator has structural advantage if in the existing plan of operation, oil or gas tend to migrate in the reservoir toward his wells. Thus with a water drive, operators located high on the structure tend to have structural advantage.

[30] In some fourteen producing states the conservation commission may order unitization of a reservoir when the owners of some specified percentage of the property interests, ranging from 60 to 85 percent, have agreed upon a plan acceptable to the commission. See McDonald, *Petroleum Conservation*, pp. 217–226.

We now need to consider possible objections—either to compulsory unitization per se or to freedom for operators under a unit plan.

OBJECTIONS TO COMPULSORY UNITIZATION PER SE

We have already indicated some of the reasons why individuals may reject voluntary unitization. In fact, these also may be reasons for resisting any move to compulsory unitization. There are additional objections to such a move.

First, some operators object to compulsion per se. No one likes to be compelled to do anything, even if it appears to be in one's interest. Nonetheless, this is a peculiar objection to compulsory unitization because the alternative is not freedom without unitization, but rather a system of rather elaborate and detailed compulsion as to well density, production rate, disposition of gas, and so forth. No one seriously denies the need for regulation in the interest of conservation. So the question is, What kind of compulsion shall we have? We recommend compulsion only with respect to unitization, and advocate complete freedom (except from environmental controls) thereafter. We interpret this to be less compulsion, not more.

Second, the unitization process is troublesome and time-consuming. Onshore, where there are often many operators and even more royalty owners, it is often difficult and highly time-consuming to work out an agreement acceptable to all. It is also common to encounter ignorance, mistrust, and conflicts of interest (for example, as between the majors and independents). Hence this objection. However, on the outer continental shelf the number of operators in a reservoir is typically small (due partly to the large size of the leases). Fewer small independents are involved, and there is only one royalty owner, who already is disposed toward unitization. Thus the objection is not very strong for unitization on the outer continental shelf, and only somewhat more so on the onshore public domain, except where private and state lands are interspersed with federal lands.

Third, there is the question of possible concentration of effective control of production. It is usual for the operator having the largest interest in a reservoir to be appointed unit manager on behalf of all the operators. This gives rise to the specter of all reservoirs being operated by the larger firms, whose interests do not necessarily coincide with those of smaller operators,[31] and who would gain additional market control. The weakness of this argument is in the implicit equation of largest interest in a reservoir with a large company. If there are many reservoirs in the leasable area, statistically a given operator, as manager, should come to control the same share of reservoirs as his share in total production. Concentration of control need not be increased. Moreover, there need be no tendency for a small bloc of companies to form a generally collusive group, since the mix of companies would vary from reservoir to reservoir. In any case, it is not clear what gain there could be to concentration of control, since not even a domestic monopolist could affect the price of oil, which is effectively set by OPEC.

Objections to Freedom for Operators Under Unitization

Even if it were agreed, as it generally is in the abstract, that unitization is desirable, some would object to granting unitized operators complete freedom as to well spacing, production rates, and the like. These objections fall under two general headings.

The Need to Prevent Physical Waste. Admittedly, the production plan adopted by a unit might involve some loss of ultimate recovery or some gas flaring, for instance. Those who equate conservation with the prevention of physical waste must therefore object to operator freedom and insist on regulations similar to those presently in operation. Not much can be said in response to this objection except to try to convince such believers that, rationally, conservation is the maximization of the value of a resource, not the "saving" of every last recoverable particle. As indicated above, the physical waste concept is based on the premise that natural resources, as compared with human and capital resources, are the only ones that need to be economized. The fact is that conservation is simply an aspect of the general problem of economizing scarce resources, and that saving a barrel of oil worth $13 at a labor and capital cost of $15 is bad economics and bad public policy.

---

[31] For instance, an integrated company with refineries to supply might choose a different rate of production in a given situation than an independent who sells his output. Or a well-capitalized major may be less concerned about current cash flow than an independent with sizable bank debt.

The Fear That the Relevant Markets Are Insufficiently Competitive.
To advocate freedom of action is to assume, as we do, that the relevant
markets (for oil and gas, capital and labor) are at least "workably"
competitive. To those who object, it may be pointed out that these
are the same markets as those which set the prices and rates of discount that would be used in determining MERs with economic content.
They are the same markets as those which guide exploration decisions,
but in this case they are not subject to regulation. As for the oil and
gas industry itself, it is one of the nation's less concentrated major
industries,[32] there is a large independent segment into which entry is
easy, its price behavior in the absence of market demand prorationing is
indicative of competition,[33] and the price of oil, effectively limited by
the world price, cannot be raised by restricting output. The anticompeti-
tive results of the industry in the past have been caused by government
action taken to reduce competition, specifically market demand prorationing and oil import limitations. With the effective removal of both
these, the industry is, we believe, more competitive than the typical
manufacturing industry.

As the foregoing suggests, we do not feel that the objections to compulsory unitization with operator freedom are sufficiently sound to
refute our arguments for it. We believe that it would contribute significantly to maximizing the value of oil and gas resources to society,
and to maximizing the capture of pure economic rent from federal
lands by the government. Perhaps emphasis should be placed chiefly on
the encouragement of voluntary unitization. It is possible that most of the
benefits we foresee would be realizable if the Department of the Interior
as lessor-regulator offered operators a choice of MER-based regulation
(with economic content) or unitization with freedom of action. In any
case, it is not feasible for the Interior Department to compel unitization
of reservoirs where state and private land is interspersed with federal
land.

It should be noted, finally, that because of the large size of outer
continental shelf leases many reservoirs are one-operator reservoirs.
They are automatically unitized. Such single operators should, we

[32] Federal Trade Commission, Economic Report, *Concentration Levels and
Trends in the Energy Sector of the U.S. Economy* (Washington, D.C., GPO,
March 1974).
[33] The usual interpretation of "market demand" prorationing is that it was
adopted as a means of restraining price competition.

believe, be free to develop and operate their reservoirs so as to maximize their value. No issue of compulsion, conflict of operator interest, or managerial cost arises here.

APPENDIX: UNOFFICIAL FORM FOR A UNIT AGREEMENT COVERING AN EXPLORATORY UNIT ON THE OUTER CONTINENTAL SHELF, UNDER CONSIDERATION BY THE U.S. GEOLOGICAL SURVEY

UNIT AGREEMENT FOR THE DEVELOPMENT AND OPERATION OF THE _____ UNIT AREA OUTER CONTINENTAL SHELF GULF OF MEXICO—OFFSHORE_____

This Agreement, entered into as of the _____ day of _____, 19_____, by and between the parties subscribing, ratifying or consenting hereto, and herein referred to as the "parties hereto,"

WITNESSETH:

WHEREAS, the parties hereto are the owners of working or other oil and gas interests in the Unit Area subject to this agreement; and

WHEREAS, the Outer Continental Shelf Lands Act of August 7, 1953, 67 Stat. 462; 43 U.S.C. 1331 et seq., hereinafter referred to as the "Act," authorizes the Secretary of the Interior, in the interest of conservation, to provide for unitization, pooling, and drilling agreements; and

WHEREAS, the rules and regulations prescribed by the Secretary of the Interior pursuant to the authority granted by the Act governing the conduct of mineral operations and development in the Outer Continental Shelf provide that such agreements may be initiated by lessees or, in the interest of conservation, may be required by the Director, U.S. Geological Survey, hereinafter referred to as the "Director" of his duly authorized representative; and

WHEREAS, the parties hereto hold sufficient interest in the _____ Unit Area covering the land hereinafter described to give reasonably effective control of operations therein; and

WHEREAS, it is deemed in the interest of conservation to unitize said interests in the Unit Area under the provisions of Section 5(a)(1) of the Act with the consent of the Secretary of the Interior or his duly authorized representative for the purpose of exploration, development, and operation of oil and gas leases.

NOW, THEREFORE, in consideration of the premises and promises herein contained, the parties hereto commit their respective interests in the below-defined Unit Area and agree severally among themselves as follows:

SECTION 1: ENABLING ACT AND REGULATIONS

The Act and all valid pertinent regulations are accepted and made a part of this Agreement, insofar as such regulations are applicable hereto.

SECTION 2: UNIT AREA

The following described land as shown on the United States Official Leasing Map, for the _____ Area _____ is hereby designated and recognized as constituting the Unit Area:

LEASE NO.   AREA AND BLOCK NUMBER   ACREAGE

(TOTAL)   _____

Exhibit "A", attached hereto and made a part thereof, is a map showing the Unit Area and the boundaries and identity of the blocks and leases in said area to the extent known to the Unit Operator. Exhibit "B" attached hereto and made a part hereof is a schedule showing to the extent known to the Unit Operator the acreage, percentage, and kind of ownership of oil and gas interests in all land in the Unit Area. "Exhibits "A" and "B" shall be revised by the Unit Operator whenever changes render such revision necessary, or when requested by the Oil and Gas Supervisor, U.S. Geological Survey, hereinafter referred to as "Supervisor," and not less than four (4) copies of the revised exhibits shall be filed with the Supervisor.

The Unit Area as described above shall, when practicable, be expanded to include therein any additional land or shall be contracted to exclude lands whenever either expansion or contraction is necessary or advisable to conform with the purposes of this Agreement.

Such expansion or contraction shall be effected in the following manner:

(a) Unit Operator, on its own motion, after preliminary concurrence of or on demand of the Conservation Manager of the Gulf of Mexico OCS Operations, hereinafter referred to as "Conservation Manager," shall prepare a notice of proposed expansion or contraction describing the contemplated changes in the boundaries of the Unit Area, the reasons therefor, and the proposed effective date thereof, preferably the first day of a month subsequent to the date of notice.

(b) Said notice shall be delivered to the Supervisor, and copies thereof mailed to the last known address of each working interest owner and lessee whose interest is affected, advising that thirty (30) days will be allowed for submission to the Unit Operator of any objections.

(c) Upon expiration of the 30-day period provided in the preceding item (b) hereof, Unit Operator shall file with the Supervisor evidence of mailing of the notices of expansion or contraction and a copy of any objections thereto which have been filed with the Unit Operator, together with an application, in sufficient number, for approval of such expansion or contraction and with appropriate joinders.

(d) After due consideration of all pertinent information, the expansion or contraction shall, upon approval by the Supervisor, become effective as of the date prescribed in the notice thereof.

(e) The leases, insofar as they cover any lands which are excluded under the provision of this Section 2, may be maintained and continued in full force and effect in accordance with the terms, provisions and conditions contained in the controlling lease or leases and amendments thereto; however, subject to the provisions of Section 9, a lessee may elect to relinquish that portion of a lease which lies outside of the Unit Area and thus terminate the obligation of paying rentals or minimum royalties on that portion of the lease.

SECTION 3: UNITIZED LAND AND UNITIZED SUBSTANCES

All land committed to this Agreement shall constitute land referred to herein as "Unitized Land" or "Unitized Acreage." All oil and gas within and produced from any and all formations of the Unitized Land are unitized under the terms of this Agreement and herein are called "Unitized Substances."

SECTION 4: UNIT OPERATOR

Except as otherwise specifically provided herein, the exclusive right, privilege, and duty of exercising any and all rights of the parties hereto which are necessary or convenient for exploring, producing, storing, allocating, and distributing the Unitized Substances are hereby delegated to and shall be exercised by the Unit Operator as herein provided.

_____ is hereby designated as Unit Operator and, by signature hereto as Unit Operator, agrees and consents to accept the duties and obligations of Unit Operator, for the discovery, development and production of Unitized Substances as herein provided. Whenever reference is made herein to Unit Operator, such reference means the Unit Operator, acting in the capacity and not as an owner of interest in Unitized Substances, and the term "Working Interest Owner," when used herein, shall include Unit Operator as the owner of a working interest when such an interest is owned by it. A change of Unit Operator may be negotiated by the owners of the working interests in Unitized Substances and four (4) executed copies of the designation of successor Unit Operator shall be filed with the Supervisor. Such designation shall not become effective until (a) a Unit Operator so designated shall accept in writing the duties and responsibilities of Unit Operator, and (b) the selection has been approved by the Supervisor.

If no successor Unit Operator is selected and qualified as herein provided, the Conservation Manager may either issue a demand that a successor Unit Operator be designated within 30 days of such demand or at his election may declare this Agreement terminated.

Section 5: Accounting Provisions and Unit Operating Agreement

If all of the working interests in the leases set out in Exhibit "B" are owned by one party, it shall pay all costs and expenses incurred by Unit Operator in conducting unit operations. If the Unit Operator is not the sole owner of working interests, costs and expenses incurred by Unit Operator in conducting unit operations shall be paid and apportioned among and borne by the owners of working interests, all in accordance with the agreement or agreements entered into by and between the Unit Operator and the owners of working interests, whether one or more, separately or collectively. Any agreement or agreements entered into between the working interest owners and the Unit Operator as provided for in this section, whether one or more, are herein referred to as the "Unit Operating Agreement." Such Unit Operating Agreement shall also provide the manner in which the working interest owners shall be entitled to receive their respective proportionate and allocated share of the benefits accruing hereto in conformity with their underlying operating agreements, leases, or other contracts, and such other rights and obligations as between Unit Operator and the working interest owners as may be agreed upon by Unit Operator and the working interest owners; however, no such Unit Operating Agreement, or any amendments thereto, shall be deemed either to modify any of the terms and conditions of this Agreement or to relieve the Unit Operator of any right or obligation established under this Agreement, and in case of any inconsistency or conflict between this Agreement and the Unit Operating Agreement, this Agreement shall govern. Three true copies of any Unit Operating

Agreement executed pursuant to this section shall be filed with the Supervisor, prior to approval of this Agreement.

SECTION 6: PLANS OF OPERATIONS

Concurrently with the filing of this Agreement for approval, Unit Operator shall submit an initial Plan of Operations prescribing an acceptable exploratory drilling program for the Unit Area. Such program shall call for the drilling of no less than _____ (   ) exploratory wells to no less than _____ feet and, when approved by the Supervisor, shall constitute the exploratory drilling obligations of the Unit Operator under this Agreement for the period of time specified in the initial plan. Each of the wells drilled thereunder will be drilled to a depth in excess of the minimum depth specified (all depths being true vertical depths) unless the Unit Operator establishes to the satisfaction of the Supervisor that a lesser depth is warranted.

Unit Operator shall commence drilling its first unit well not later than six (6) months following the approval of the Initial Plan of Operations, and shall continue drilling diligently, allowing not more than six (6) months to elapse between the completion of drilling operations on one well and the beginning of the next well, until drilling operations at all wells in the Initial Plan of Operations have been completed. The Initial Plan of Operations shall expire not later than six (6) months following the completion of _____ (   ) wells.

No later than thirty (30) days prior to the expiration of the Initial Plan of Operations, or any approved supplemental plan thereto, the Unit Operator shall submit, to the Supervisor, an acceptable Plan of Operations for the Unit Area which, when approved by the Supervisor, shall constitute the further exploratory and/or development drilling and operating obligations of the Unit Operator under this Agreement for the period specified therein. No exploratory or development drilling operations shall be conducted within the Unit Area other than as provided for in an approved Plan of Operations.

Any plan submitted shall provide for the exploration of the Unit Area and for the diligent drilling necessary for the determination of lands thereof capable of producing Unitized Substances in paying quantities in each and every productive formation. All plans shall be as complete and adequate as the Supervisor may determine necessary to provide timely exploration and development of the Unit Area to ensure proper conservation of its oil and gas resources. Such plans shall (a) specify the number and general location of each well including surface and projected bottom hole location for directionally drilled wells, (b) specify the proposed order and time for drilling each well, (c) to the extent practicable, specify the operating practices regarded as necessary and advisable for proper conservation of natural resources and protection of the environment, and (d) when deemed necessary by the Supervisor, present documented evidence of further negotiations and/or contract arrangements which have a direct bearing on the diligent prosecution of said plan.

Reasonable diligence shall be exercised in complying with the obligations of an approved Plan of Operations. The Supervisor is authorized to grant a reasonable extension of any or all of the critical dates for exploratory drilling operations cited in the Initial or subsequent Plans of Operations where such action is justified because of unusual conditions or circumstances; however, no such extension shall exceed a period of four (4) months for each well required by the Initial Plan of Operations.

The failure of the Unit Operator to timely drill any of the wells provided for in a Plan of Operations required under this Section or to timely submit an acceptable Plan of Operations for approval by the Supervisor or in any way to timely comply with the requirements of this Agreement shall result in the Unit Operator being deemed in default and shall result in the automatic elimination from this Agreement all ¼–¼ blocks of land, no part of which is entitled to be within a Participating Area on the date of default, effective as of the date of default. Should there be no Participating Area in existence on the effective date of default, this Agreement shall automatically terminate as of the date of default.

Separate plans may be submitted for separate productive zones, subject to the approval of the Supervisor. Said plan or plans shall be modified or supplemented when necessary to meet changed conditions or to protect the interest of all parties to this Agreement.

SECTION 7: PARTICIPATING AREA

Upon completion of a well capable of producing Unitized Substances in paying quantities or as soon thereafter as required by the Supervisor, the Unit Operator shall submit, to the Supervisor for approval, a schedule of all land then regarded as reasonably proved to be productive of Unitized Substances in paying quantities; a well capable of producing Unitized Substances in paying quantities shall be defined as a well capable of producing Unitized Substances in quantities sufficient to yield a return in excess of drilling and production costs; such a determination shall be subject to review and approval of the Supervisor. All lands in said schedule, upon approval thereof by the Supervisor, shall constitute the Participating Area effective as of the date such production commences or the effective date of this Unit Agreement, whichever is later. Said schedule shall also set forth the percentage of Unitized Substances to be allocated as herein provided to each tract in the Participating Area so established, and shall govern the allocation of unitized production commencing as of effective date of the Participating Area. A separate participating area may be established for each separate pool of Unitized Substances or for any group thereof which is produced as a single pool or zone and any two or more Participating Areas so established may be combined into one, all subject to approval of the Supervisor. Subject to like approval, the Participating Area or areas so established shall be revised from time to time to include additional land then regarded as reasonably proved to be productive or necessary to unit operations, or to exclude land then regarded as reasonably proved not to be productive or not necessary to unit operations, and the schedule of allocation percentages shall be revised accordingly. The effective date of any revision shall be the first of the month in which is obtained the knowledge of information on which such revision is predicated; provided, however, that a more appropriate effective date may be used if justified by the Unit Operator and approved by the Supervisor. No land shall be excluded from the Participating Area on account of depletion of the Unitized Substances.

Nothing herein contained shall be construed as requiring any retroactive adjustment for production obtained prior to the effective date of the revision of the Participating Area.

SECTION 8: ALLOCATION OF PRODUCTION

All Unitized Substances produced from a Participating Area established under this Agreement, except any part thereof used in conformity with good operating practices within the Unit Area for drilling, operating, camp and other production or development purposes, or for repressuring or recycling in accordance with a Plan of Operations approved by the Supervisor, or unavoidably lost, shall be deemed to be produced equally on an acreage basis from the several tracts of Unitized Land of the Participating Area established for such production. For the purpose of determining any benefits accruing under this Agreement, each such tract of Unitized Land shall have allocated to it such percentage of said production as the number of acres of such tract included in said Participating Area bears to the total number of acres of Unitized Land in said Participating Area and royalty due thereon shall be paid by the Unit Operator. Allocation of production hereunder for purposes other than for settlement of the royalty obligations of the respective working interest owners, shall be on the basis prescribed in the Unit Operating Agreement whether in conformity with the basis of allocation herein set forth or otherwise. It is hereby agreed that production of Unitized Substances from a Participating Area shall be allocated as provided herein regardless of whether any well or wells are drilled on any particular part or tract of said Participating Area.

SECTION 9: RELINQUISHMENT OF LEASES

Pursuant to the provisions of the leases and 43 CFR 3306.1, a lessee of record shall, subject to the provisions of the Unit Operating Agreement, have the right to relinquish any or all leases committed hereto, in whole or in part; Provided, however, that no relinquishment shall be made of land within a Participating Area without the prior approval of the Supervisor. Upon such relinquishment the Unit Area shall be contracted automatically to exclude the relinquished land, as of the date of relinquishment.

SECTION 10: RENTALS AND MINIMUM ROYALTIES

Rentals on nonproductive lands are payable prior to the beginning of each year. Minimum royalties accrue as of the first of each lease year and are payable at the end of the lease year. Beginning with the lease year commencing on or after _____ and for each lease year thereafter, rentals and minimum royalty payments shall be made on the following basis:

A. An advance annual rental, equal to that amount called for in the individual leases involved but in no case less than $3.00 an acre or fraction thereof and in no event creditable against production royalties, shall be paid for all acreage within the Unit Area except for that acreage comprising those individual lease tracts which are credited with a production allocation through a Participating Area.

B. An annual minimum royalty, equal to that amount called for in the individual leases involved but in no case less than $3.00 an acre or fraction thereof, shall accrue at the beginning of each lease year for all Unitized Acreage within a Participating Area as of the beginning of the lease year. The deficit, if any, between the actual royalty paid on production and the minimum royalty prescribed herein shall be payable at the expiration of the lease year.

SECTION 11: AUTOMATIC CONTRACTION OF UNIT AREA

All ¼–¼ blocks of land, no part of which is entitled to be within a Participating Area on the _____ anniversary of the effective date of the initial Participating Area established under this Agreement, shall be eliminated automatically from this Agreement effective as of said _____ anniversary and such lands shall no longer be a part of the Unit Area and shall no longer be subject to this Agreement unless diligent drilling operations are in progress on an exploratory well on said _____ anniversary, in which event all such lands shall remain subject hereto for so long as such drilling operations are continued diligently with not more than 6 months time elapsing between the completion of one exploratory well and the commencement of the next exploratory well. For the purposes of this section, an exploratory well is any well approved by the Supervisor as such and drilled either (a) in search of a new and as yet undiscovered commercial petroleum deposit or (b) with the hope of greatly extending the limits of an existing Participating Area. If Unit Operator has completed the drilling of an exploratory well during the six (6) months immediately preceding said _____ anniversary under an approved Plan of Operations, lands not entitled to be within the participating area shall not be eliminated from this Agreement on said _____ anniversary if the drilling of another exploratory well is commenced under an approved Plan of Operations within six (6) months of the completion of said well, and the lands not credited to be in participation shall remain subject hereto so long as exploratory drilling operations are continued diligently with not more than six (6) months elapsing between the completion of drilling operations of one exploratory well and the commencement of the next exploratory well. With prior approval of the Supervisor, a period of time in excess of six (6) months may, when warranted, be allowed to elapse between the completion of one well and the commencement of the next well without the automatic elimination of nonparticipating acreage.

Unitized Lands found to be capable of production in paying quantities by drilling operations which serve to delay automatic elimination of lands under this section shall be incorporated into a Participating Area in the same manner as such lands would have been incorporated in such areas had such lands been found to be capable of production in paying quantities prior to said _____ anniversary. In the event nonparticipating lands are retained under this Agreement after the _____ anniversary of the initial Participating Area as a result of drilling operations on lands not entitled to participation, all ¼–¼ blocks of land, no part of which is entitled to be within a Participating Area, shall be eliminated automatically as of the 181st day, or such later date as may be established by the Supervisor, following the completion of drilling operations of the last well recognized as delaying such automatic elimination beyond the _____ anniversary of the initial Participating Area established under this Agreement.

The leases, as to any lands excluded from this Agreement in accordance with this Section, shall be governed by the terms and provisions of said leases and other instruments affecting the separate leases involved.

SECTION 12: LEASES AND CONTRACTS CONFORMED AND EXTENDED

The terms, conditions and provisions of all leases, subleases and other contracts relating to exploration, drilling, development, or operations for oil or gas on lands committed to this Agreement, are hereby expressly modified and amended only to the extent necessary to make the same conform to the provisions hereof, but otherwise to remain in full force and effect. The Supervisor by his approval hereof, does hereby establish, alter, suspend, change, or revoke the drilling, production, rental, minimum royalty and royalty requirements of the Federal leases committed hereto and the regulations in respect thereto, to conform said requirements to the provisions of this Agreement, and, without limiting the generality of the foregoing, all leases, subleases, and contracts are particularly modified in accordance with the following:

A. Drilling and producing operations performed hereunder upon any submerged Unitized Lands will be accepted and deemed to be performed upon and for the benefit of the entire Unit Area, and no lease shall be deemed to expire by reason of failure to drill or produce wells situated on the tracts therein embraced.

B. Suspension of drilling or producing operations on all Unitized Lands pursuant to direction or consent of the Secretary, or his duly authorized representative, shall be deemed to constitute such suspension pursuant to such direction or consent as to each and every tract of Unitized Lands; however, a suspension of drilling and producing operations on specified lands shall be applicable only to such lands.

C. In the event oil or gas is discovered on lands subject to this Agreement, any lease committed hereto shall, as to the Unitized Lands, continue in force beyond the term so provided therein, or as extended by law, for so long as oil or gas may be produced from Unitized Lands in paying quantities, or drilling or well reworking operations, as approved by the Secretary or his duly authorized representative, are conducted thereon. This subsection shall not operate to extend any lease or portion thereof as to lands excluded from this Agreement by the contraction of the Unit Area. Upon termination of this Agreement, the leases covered hereby may be maintained and continued in full force and effect in accordance with the terms, provisions, and conditions of the lease or leases and amendments thereto.

SECTION 13: EFFECTIVE DATE AND TERM

This Agreement shall become effective upon approval by the Secretary or his duly authorized representative and shall terminate _____ ( ) years from said effective date unless,

(a) Such date of expiration is extended by the Director; or

(b) Unitized Substances are produced from wells drilled hereunder, in which event this Agreement shall remain in effect so long as Unitized Substances may be produced in quantities sufficient to yield a return in excess of current operating costs or drilling or well reworking operations, pursuant to 30 CFR 250.35, are being conducted hereunder; or

(c) It is terminated as heretofore provided in this Agreement.

This Agreement may be terminated at any time by the owners of a majority of the working interests, on an acreage basis, with the approval of the Supervisor. Notice of any such approval shall be given by the Unit Operator to all parties hereto.

SECTION 14: APPEARANCES

Unit Operator shall, after notice to other parties affected, have the right to appear for and on behalf of any and all interested parties affected hereby before the Department of the Interior, and to appeal from orders issued under the regulations of said Department, or to apply for relief from any of said regulations or in any proceedings relative to operations before the Department of the Interior or any other legally constituted authority; provided, however, that any interested party shall also have the right at its own expense to be heard in any such proceeding.

SECTION 15: NO WAIVER OF CERTAIN RIGHTS

Nothing contained in this Agreement shall be construed as a waiver by any party hereto of the right to assert any legal or constitutional right or defense pertaining to the validity or invalidity of any law of the United States, or regulations issued thereunder, in any way affecting such party or as a waiver by any such party of any right beyond his or its authority to waive.

SECTION 16: UNAVOIDABLE DELAY

All obligations imposed by this Agreement requiring Unit Operator to commence or continue drilling or to operate on or produce Unitized Substances from any of the lands covered by this Agreement, shall be suspended while, but only so long as, Unit Operator, despite the exercise of due care and diligence, is prevented from complying with such obligations, in whole or in part, by strikes, Acts of God, Federal or other applicable law, Federal or other authorized governmental agencies, unavoidable accidents, uncontrollable delays in transportation, inability to obtain necessary materials in open market, or other matters beyond the reasonable control of Unit Operator, whether similar to matters herein enumerated or not.

No obligation which is suspended under this section shall become due less than thirty (30) days after it has been determined that the suspension is no longer applicable. Determination of creditable "Unavoidable Delay" time shall be made by the Unit Operator subject to the approval of the Director. Notwithstanding any other provisions of this agreement, the Director, on his own initiative or upon appropriate justification by Unit Operator, may postpone any obligation under this agreement to commence or continue drilling or to operate on or produce Unitized Substances from lands covered by this Agreement when in his judgment circumstances warrant such action.

SECTION 17: NONDISCRIMINATION

In connection with the performance of work under this Agreement, the Operator agrees to comply with all of the provisions of Section 202 (1) to (7) inclusive, of Executive Order 11246 (30 F.R. 12319), as amended, which are hereby incorporated by reference in this Agreement.

SECTION 18: COUNTERPARTS

This Agreement may be executed in any number of counterparts no one of which needs to be executed by all parties, or may be ratified or consented to by separate instruments in writing specifically referring hereto, and shall be binding upon all parties who have executed such a counterpart, ratification or consent hereto, with the same force and effect as if all such parties had signed the same document.

SECTION 19: SUBSEQUENT JOINDER

Any oil or gas interests in submerged lands within the Unit Area not committed hereto prior to approval of this Agreement may thereafter be committed hereto by the owner or owners thereof subscribing or consenting to this Agreement, and, if the interest is a working interest, by the owner of such interest also subscribing to the Unit Operating Agreement. The right of subsequent joinder, as provided in this Section, by a Working Interest Owner is subject to such requirements or approvals, if any, pertaining to such joinder, as may be provided for in the Unit Operating Agreement. Joinder to this Agreement by a Working Interest Owner, at any time, must be accompanied by appropriate joinder to the Unit Operating Agreement, if more than one committed Working Interest Owner is involved, in order for the interest to be regarded as committed to this Agreement. Except as may otherwise herein be provided, subsequent joinders to this Agreement shall be effective as of the first day of the month following the filing with the Supervisor of duly executed counterparts of all or any papers necessary to establish effective commitment of any tract to this Agreement unless objection to such joinder is duly made within sixty (60) days by the Supervisor.

SECTION 20: COVENANTS RUN WITH THE LAND

The covenants herein shall be construed to be covenants running with the land with respect to the interest of the parties hereto and their successors in interest until this Agreement terminates, and any grant, transfer or conveyance, of interest in land or leases subject hereto shall be and hereby is conditioned upon the assumption of all privileges and obligations hereunder by the grantee, transferee, or other successor in interest. No assignment or transfer of any working interest or other interest subject hereto shall be binding upon Unit Operator until the first day of the calendar month after Unit Operator is furnished with the original, photostatic or certified copy of the instrument of transfer.

SECTION 21: NOTICE

All notices, demands or statements required hereunder to be given or rendered to the parties hereto shall be deemed fully given if given in writing and personally delivered to the party or sent by post paid registered or certified mail, addressed to such party or parties at their respective addresses set forth in connection with the signatures hereto or to such other address as any such party may have furnished in writing to the party sending the notice, demand or statement.

IN WITNESS WHEREOF, the parties hereto have caused this agreement to be executed and have set opposite their respective names the date of execution.

UNIT OPERATOR
(AS UNIT OPERATOR AND AS
WORKING INTEREST OWNER)

WITNESSES:

_____

BY _____

Its Attorney-in-Fact

DATE:

WITNESSES:

WORKING INTEREST OWNERS

_____

BY _____

BY _____

8

Environmental Regulation

In chapters 3 and 4 we indicated that, for the government to derive the maximum of pure economic rent from federal lands, there should be regulation of lessees to internalize externalities such as environmental damage from minerals production. This means some sacrifice in revenues from leasable lands, but a gain in social welfare. To ignore environmental damage in the interest of maximizing revenues is the equivalent of levying a differential excise tax on environmental amenities, with a consequent distortion of production at the expense of such amenities in favor of minerals production.

In this chapter we examine the different kinds of environmental regulation of federal lessees in minerals production with a view to evaluating them as means of efficiently internalizing externalities. It will be sufficient to indicate the nature of such regulation if we confine ourselves to outer continental shelf oil and gas regulations, coal regulations, and shale oil regulations. The first two are set out in general operating regulations; the third in the lease contract for shale oil production. In presenting these regulations we shall employ quotations extensively, for paraphrasing introduces the risk of misinterpretation of some very precise stipulations.

OUTER CONTINENTAL SHELF OIL AND GAS OPERATIONS

In general, environmental regulations for outer continental shelf oil and gas are designed to prevent the interchange of fluids between strata in the drilling, operation, or abandonment of wells, to prevent oil spills;

154

and to ensure proper correction of any environmental damage accidentally incurred. With respect to the drilling of wells:

> The lessee shall take all necessary precautions to keep all wells under control at all times. . . . The design of the integrated casing, cementing, drilling mud, and blowout prevention program shall be based upon sound engineering principles, and must take into account the depths at which various fluid or mineral-bearing formations are expected to be penetrated, and the formation fracture gradients and pressures expected to be encountered, and other pertinent geologic and engineering data and information about the area.[1]

> The lessee shall case and cement all wells with a sufficient number of strings of casing in a manner necessary to: (i) prevent release of fluids from any stratum through the well bore (directly or indirectly) into the sea; (ii) prevent communication between separate hydrocarbon-bearing strata (except such strata approved for commingling) and between hydrocarbon and water-bearing strata; (iii) prevent contamination of fresh water strata, gas, or water. . . . The lessee shall install casing necessary to withstand collapse, bursting, tensile, and other stresses and the casing shall be cemented in a manner which will anchor and support the casing.[2]

> The lessee shall maintain readily accessible for use quantities of mud sufficient to insure well control. The testing procedures, characteristics, and use of drilling procedures shall be such as are necessary to prevent blowouts.[3]

(A "blowout" is an uncontrolled discharge of oil under pressure from the reservoir through or in the neighborhood of the well bore. A blowout spills oil into the sea and may contaminate the underground freshwater-bearing strata.)

> The lessee shall install, use, and test blowout preventers and related well-control equipment in a manner necessary to prevent blowouts. Such installation, use and testing must meet the standards or requirements prescribed by the supervisor. . . . Blowout preventers and related well-control equipment shall be pressure tested when installed, after each string of casing is cemented, and at such other times as prescribed by the supervisor. Blowout preventers shall be activated frequently to test for proper functioning as prescribed by the supervisor.[4]

[1] 30 CFR 250.41(a).
[2] 30 CFR 250.41(a)(1).
[3] 30 CFR 250.41(a)(2).
[4] 30 CFR 250.41(a)(3). The supervisor referred to here is the area oil and gas supervisor, Conservation Division, Geological Survey.

The lessee shall: (1) in wells capable of flowing oil or gas, when required by the supervisor, install and maintain in operating condition storm chokes or similar subsurface safety devices; (2) for producing wells not capable of flowing oil or gas, install and maintain surface safety valves with automatic shut-down controls; and (3) periodically test or inspect such devices or equipment as prescribed by the supervisor.[5]

(A storm choke is a device to shut off the flow from a well should surface control equipment be destroyed or damaged. In the absence of such a device an oil spill may result from an explosion, a fire, or storm damage at the surface.)

With respect to pollution and waste disposal:

The lessee shall not pollute land or water or damage the aquatic life of the sea or allow extraneous matter to enter and damage any mineral- or water-bearing formation. The lessee shall dispose of all liquid and non-liquid waste materials as prescribed by the supervisor. All spills or leakage of oil or waste materials shall be recorded by the lessee and, upon request of the supervisor, shall be reported to him. All spills or leakage of a substantial size or quantity, as defined by the supervisor, and those of any size or quantity which cannot be immediately controlled also shall be reported by the lessee without delay to the supervisor and to the Coast Guard and the Regional Director of the Federal Water Pollution Control Administration.[6]

If the waters of the sea are polluted by the drilling or production operations conducted by or on behalf of the lessee, and such pollution damages or threatens to damage aquatic life, wildlife, or public or private property, the control and total removal of the pollutant, wheresoever found, proximately resulting therefrom shall be at the expense of the lessee. Upon failure of the lessee to control and remove the pollutant the supervisor, in cooperation with other appropriate agencies of the Federal, State and local governments, or in cooperation with the lessee, or both, shall have the right to accomplish the control and removal of the pollutant in accordance with any established contingency plan for combating oil spills or by other means at the cost of the lessee. Such action shall not relieve the lessee of any responsibility as provided herein.[7]

Note that the liability for cleaning up pollutants, or bearing the expense thereof, is not limited in any way. We shall have more to say

[5] 30 CFR 250.41(b).
[6] 30 CFR 250.43(a).
[7] 30 CFR 250.43(b).

on this at a later point. The regulation states, "The lessee shall promptly plug and abandon any well on the leased land that is not used or useful. . . . No well shall be plugged and abandoned until the manner and method of plugging shall be approved or prescribed by the supervisor. Equipment shall be removed, and premises at the well-site shall be properly conditioned immediately after plugging operations are completed on any well when directed by the supervisor."[8] (A well not properly plugged upon abandonment may allow pollutants to flow into the sea or to invade the freshwater-bearing strata beneath the surface.)

We shall not review environmental regulations of onshore oil and gas operations. They are generally equivalent to or consistent with those for outer continental shelf operations, but less emphasis is placed on control of oil spills and more on cleaning up and restoring the land surface after well abandonment.[9]

COAL OPERATIONS

When an area (of federal lands) is initially considered for coal development, the relevant regulations require the authorized officer to make an environmental impact assessment. Prior to the selection of tracts for leasing he must:

> . . . Evaluate the potential effects of all phases of such coal development on the environment, including fish and other aquatic resources, wildlife habitats and populations, aesthetics, recreation, cultural, and other resources in the affected area. This evaluation shall take into account alternative uses of the land and its other natural resources, the need for the proposed coal development, and the socioeconomic considerations relevant to multiple-use management principles.[10]

If it is determined that the decision to lease would be "a major Federal action significantly affecting the quality of the human environment," then an environmental impact statement must be prepared.[11] If a decision is made to offer tracts for leasing, the authorized officer may

[8] 30 CFR 250.44.
[9] See 30 CFR 221.21-221.37.
[10] 43 CFR 3041.0-6(b).
[11] This is required by the National Environmental Policy Act of 1969 (42 U.S.C. 4321 et seq.).

"develop and include in such offer such specific terms and conditions as may be required by specific local conditions to protect the environment, to permit use of the land for other purposes, to allow new post-mining land uses, and to protect other resources."[12]

Under the regulations, the operator who accepts a coal lease shall:

(1) Conduct surface coal mining operations so as to maximize the extraction of the coal resource so that future disturbance through the resumption of mining will be minimized.

(2) Reclaim the land affected, as contemporaneously as practicable with operations, to a condition at least fully capable of supporting all actual or practicable uses which it was capable of supporting prior to any exploration or mining, or equal or better uses that can reasonably be attained.

(3) Replace overburden and waste materials in the mineral area by backfilling, . . . grading or other means so as, to the maximum extent practicable, to restore the approximate original contour and to eliminate high walls and spoil piles. Where the thickness of the coal deposits relative to the volume of overburden is large or where the overburden and other spoil waste materials are either insufficient or more than sufficient to restore the approximate original contour, the operator shall backfill, grade, and compact, using all available overburden or spoil material to obtain the lowest practicable grade . . . in order to provide adequate drainage and to cover all acid-forming or other toxic materials.

(4) Stabilize and protect all surface area, including spoil piles . . . to effectively control slides, erosion subsidence and attendant air and water pollution.

(5) Remove the top soil separately, replace it on the backfill area or, if not utilized immediately segregate it in a separate pile from other spoil [and protect it with a view to restoring it with covered vegetation].

(6) Insure that [water impoundments do not, among other things,] adversely affect the water resources utilized by adjacent or surrounding landowners for agricultural, industrial, recreational, or domestic uses.

(7) Cover or plug all auger mine holes . . . in order to minimize or prevent harmful drainage.

(8) Minimize disturbances to the prevailing quality and quantity of water in surface and groundwater systems.

(9) Place all waste piles in areas designated in the approved mining plan and stabilize them, . . . shape the waste pile to be compatible with natural surroundings and terrain, cover with topsoil or other suitable material [in accordance with paragraph (4) above].

---

[12] 43 CFR 3041.0-6(c) and (e).

(10) Refrain from surface coal mining within 200 feet of active and abandoned underground mines.

(11) Incorporate sound engineering standards and practices for the design, construction and use of impoundments for the disposal of [wastes].

(12) Treat or dispose of all rubbish and noxious substances in a manner designed to prevent air and water pollution and fire hazards [and dispose of solid waste with the same view].

(13) Use explosives only in accordance with existing Federal and State laws and the conditions specified by the Mining Supervisor.

(14) Construct, maintain, and, when they are no longer necessary, remove roads, pipelines, power lines, and similar utility access facilities . . . in a manner that will prevent to the maximum extent practicable erosion and siltation, pollution of water, damage to fish or wildlife or their habitats, or public or private property.

(15) Refrain from constructing roads or other access ways in or near stream beds or drainage channels that would seriously alter the normal flow of water therein.

(16) Except where other reclamation is expressly provided for in an approved mining plan, establish on the regraded areas and all other affected lands a diverse vegetation cover . . . at least equal in density and permanence to the natural vegetation.

(17) Assume responsibility for successful revegetation.

(18) Allow access to and upon the affected Federal land . . . for all lawful and proper purposes, except where such access would unduly interfere with the authorized use or would constitute a hazard to public health and safety.

(19) Regulate public access, vehicular traffic, and wildlife or livestock grazing to protect the public, wildlife, and livestock from hazards associated with the operations and to protect the revegetated areas from unplanned and uncontrolled grazing.

(20) Substantially backfill, fence, protect, or otherwise effectively close all surface openings, auger holes, subsidence holes, surface excavations or workings which are a hazard to people or animals.[13]

With respect to the surface effects of underground mining, the regulations state that each operator shall:

(1) Adopt measures consistent with feasible known technology in order to prevent or control subsidence, maximize mine stability, and maintain the value and use of surface lands.

(2) [Leave pillars or panels of adequate dimensions] to assure surface stability.

[13] 43 CFR 3041.0-7(b)(1)-(20).

(3) Install [if required by the Mining Supervisor] a subsidence monitoring system.[14]

Further, in planning and operations, the operator shall take into account visual resources, employ measures to protect fish and wildlife, and conduct operations affecting cultural and scientific resources in accordance with lease terms and the approved mining plan.[15]

To assure compliance with the above requirements, the operator must secure approval of a preliminary mining plan, including measures proposed to protect the environment, and post a compliance or performance bond the amount of which is set by the authorized officer (of the Geological Survey).[16]

The foregoing quotations are from regulations governing surface management in connection with the development and use of federal coal resources. The relevant coal mine-operating regulations largely repeat the provisions quoted,[17] provide detailed requirements for mining plans,[18] specify abandonment procedures,[19] and summarize requirements as follows:

The operator shall take such action as may be needed to minimize, control and to the maximum extent practicable, avoid (1) soil erosion; (2) pollution of air; (3) pollution of surface or ground water; (4) serious diminution of the normal flow of water; (5) permanent damage to vegetative growth, crops or timber; (6) injury or destruction of fish and wildlife in their habitat; (7) creation of unsafe or hazardous conditions; (8) damage to improvements, whether owned by the United States, its permittees, licensees, or lessees, or by others; and (9) damage to recreational, scenic, historical, and archaeological values of the land. The surface of leased or permit lands shall be reclaimed as contemporaneously as practicable with the mining operations and in accordance with the terms and conditions prescribed in the lease, permit, or license and the provisions of the approved mining or exploration plan.[20]

---

[14] 43 CFR 3041.0-7(e)(1)-(3).

[15] 43 CFR 3041.0-7(f)-(h).

[16] 43 CFR 3041.1-1 through 3041.4.

[17] 30 CFR 211.40.

[18] 30 CFR 211.10.

[19] 30 CFR 211.41.

[20] 30 CFR 211.4(c). These regulations appear to be generally consistent with the relevant provisions of the Surface Mining Control and Reclamation Act of 1977, Public Law 95-87, 91 Stat. 445.

OIL SHALE OPERATIONS

There are no general regulations governing oil shale operations. Provisions for environmental protection in connection with such operations are included in the lease contract. The contract currently in use contains general requirements and has attached a long list of environmental stipulations. The general requirements are that:

(a) The Lessee shall conduct all operations under this lease in compliance with all applicable Federal, State and local water pollution control, water quality, air pollution control, air quality, noise control, and land reclamation statutes, regulations and standards.

(b) The Lessee shall avoid, or where avoidance is impracticable, minimize and, where practicable, repair damage to the environment, including the land, the water and air.

(c) The Oil Shale Lease Environmental Stipulations are attached to and specifically incorporated in this lease. A breach of any term of these stipulations will be a breach of the terms of this lease and subject to all the provisions of this lease with respect to remedies in case of default.[21]

(The remedies provided are suspension of operations by the lessor or the institution of court proceedings to cancel the lease.[22])

The first section of the specific environmental stipulations contains general provisions. These stipulate that environmental controls apply to not only the lessee, but also to his agents, employees, contractors, and subcontractors, and to other employees; that the controls provided for are based on existing knowledge and technology and may be changed as these change; that the lessee "shall compile data to determine the conditions existing prior to any development operations under the lease and shall . . . conduct a monitoring program before, during and subsequent to development operations" with a view to detecting, measuring, and giving timely notice of environmental damage. In collecting baseline data, the lessee must construct gauging stations on the major drainages of the leased lands, both upstream and downstream from the lands, drill a test well and install an observation well in each water-bearing zone defined by the test well; monitor air quality over at least 90 percent of each

---

[21] U.S. Department of the Interior, Bureau of Land Management, *Oil Shale Lease*, Serial no. C-20341, Tract C-b., § 11.
[22] Ibid., § 29.

lease year, using four strategically located stations; make studies of the flora and fauna of the leased lands and surrounding lands within one mile; conduct a soil survey and productivity assessment of all lands proposed to be disturbed; include an environmental monitoring program in the detailed development plans required to be approved by the mining supervisor; and submit annual reports to the supervisor on the results of the monitoring program.[23]

Section 2 of the environmental stipulations covers access and service plans. The lessee must secure approval of the mining supervisor of corridor plans for roads, pipelines, and utilities incorporating specific features to protect the environment. It is also stipulated that "the Lessee shall divert runoff from roads and uphill slopes by means of waterbars, waterbreaks, or culverts constructed in accordance with Bureau specifications."[24] With respect to oil pipelines, the lessee must provide for automatic shut-off valves necessary to prevent spills in view of "terrain and drainage systems traversed; population centers; wildlife and fishery habitat; public water supplies and significant water bodies; hazardous geologic areas; and scenic values."[25] Pipelines must correspond to detailed plans, approved by the supervisor, "for corrosive-resistant design and methods of early detection of pipeline corrosion."[26]

Regarding fire prevention and control, "The Lessee shall comply with the instructions and directions of the Mining Supervisor concerning the use, prevention and suppression of fires, and shall make every reasonable effort to prevent, control and suppress any fire on land subject to the lease. Uncontrolled fires must be immediately reported to the Mining Supervisor."[27] The lessee must construct fire lanes or perform clearing where deemed necessary by the supervisor, and must comply with National Fire Codes when handling flammables.[28]

> The control and suppression of any fires on the Leased Lands (or on adjoining public lands which have spread from the Leased Lands) caused by the Lessee or his employees, contractors, sub-contractors, or agents shall be at the expense of the Lessee. Upon the failure of the Lessee to control and suppress such fires in a manner satisfactory to him, the Mining Supervisor shall take such steps as are necessary to control and

[23] *Oil Shale Lease*, Environmental Stipulations, § 1.
[24] Ibid., § 2.
[25] Ibid.
[26] Ibid.
[27] Ibid., § 3(A)(1).
[28] Ibid., § 3(A)(2).

suppress the fire . . . and the cost of such control and suppression shall be borne by the Lessee.[29]

The Lessee shall submit for approval by the Mining Supervisor, as part of the exploration and mining plan, a detailed fish and wildlife management plan which shall include the steps which the Lessee shall take to: (1) avoid or, where avoidance is impracticable, minimize damage to fish and wildlife habitat including water supplies; (2) restore such habitat in the event it is unavoidably destroyed or damaged; (3) provide alternate habitats; and (4) provide controlled access to the public for the enjoyment of the wildlife resources on such lands as may be mutually agreed upon.[30]

Prior to construction or mining, the lessee must conduct "a thorough and professional investigation" of the leased lands for objects of historic or scientific interest, "including, but not limited to, Indian ruins, pictographs and other archaeological remains." He must report his findings to the supervisor and must not in his operations "appropriate, remove, injure, deface, or alter any object of antiquity, or of historic, prehistoric, or scientific interest."[31]

The lessee must submit oil spill contingency plans to the supervisor. The plans must also:

(1) include a description of positive spill prevention efforts which the lessee shall make; (2) include provisions for spill control; (3) provide for immediate corrective action including spill control and restoration of the affected resource; (4) provide that the Mining Supervisor shall approve any materials or devices used for spill control and shall approve any disposal sites or techniques selected to handle spilled matters; and (5) include separate and specific techniques and schedules for cleanup of spills on land, rivers and streams.[32]

The lessee must promptly report spills to the supervisor and other interested federal and state officials. Control, cleanup, and so forth are the responsibility of the lessee. If the lessee fails to perform satisfactorily the supervisor may take such measures as he deems appropriate, but "at the full expense of the Lessee."[33] The lessee may not use pesticides and herbicides without the approval of the supervisor.[34]

[29] Ibid., § 3(B).
[30] Ibid., § 4(A).
[31] Ibid., § 6.
[32] Ibid., § 7(A).
[33] Ibid., § 7(A)-(B).
[34] Ibid., § 7(E).

The lessee must avoid, or where avoidance is impracticable, minimize air pollution, including the creation of "dust problems." "The Lessee shall not burn waste, timber, or debris, except when disposal is essential and other methods of disposal would be more harmful to the environment and when authorized by the Mining Supervisor."[35]

The lessee must also avoid, or minimize, water pollution. He may not discharge waste water into any aquifer deemed by the supervisor "to be a potentially valuable water supply nor into any aquifer which will discharge the waste into a surface stream."[36]

In areas where overburden, water, or waste from mines or processing plants might contain toxic or saline materials, the Lessee shall:

(1) Divert surface or ground water so as to avoid the formation of toxic and saline water and its drainage into streams;

(2) Dispose of refuse and spent shale from mining and processing in a manner which will avoid the discharge of toxic drainage or saline water into surface or ground water;

(3) Employ, upon termination of operations, . . . all practicable closing measures . . . to avoid the formation and discharge of toxic or saline water;

(4) Dispose of toxic and saline water . . . in a manner that does not pollute surface or ground water;

(5) During mining operations, monitor spoil and refuse for the presence of materials likely to yield unacceptable alkaline, acidic, saline, or toxic solutes; and

(6) Reinject *no* water, except in compliance with Federal and State standards then in effect and where authorized to do so by the Mining Supervisor.[37]

The lessee must comply with all federal and state standards on noise pollution and must in general "keep noise at or below levels safe and acceptable for humans."[38]

Also, it is required that "the Lessee shall, in accordance with approved plans, rehabilitate all affected lands to a usable and productive condition consistent with or equal to pre-existing land uses in the area and compatible with existing, adjacent undisturbed natural areas."[39] The lessee

---

[35] Ibid., § 8.
[36] Ibid., § 9(A).
[37] Ibid., § 9(C).
[38] Ibid., § 10.
[39] Ibid., § 11(A).

must stabilize all disturbed areas by such means as "seeding; planting; mulching; and the placement of mat binders, soil binders, rock or gravel blankets or other such structures."[40] He must, where feasible, utilize waste rock from mining operations for road beds, fills and the like. He must, unless otherwise directed by the supervisor, "backfill, level, final grade, cover with topsoil and initiate vegetation of each segment of the operation area in accordance with the rehabilitation plan as soon as that segment is no longer needed."[41] He must restore vegetation of disturbed areas "by reestablishing permanent vegetation of a quality which will support fauna of the same kinds and in the same numbers as those existing at the time the base line data was obtained."[42]

Scenic values must be preserved by such means as "contours compatible with the natural environment," use of natural colors in painting facilities, and use of "natural openings" for construction.[43] Also, "the Lessee may clear and strip [of vegetation] only such land as is necessary for mining, processing, disposal, and other operations under the lease."[44]

With regard to mine waste, the lessee must "backfill or reclaim excavated material and spent shale and shall compact it thoroughly by machinery to avoid or, where avoidance is impossible, minimize erosion."[45] Other waste must be recycled or disposed of in sanitary land fills or other disposal areas. It is stipulated that "the Lessee shall select and prepare disposal sites for wastes so as to avoid downward percolation of leached products and other pollutants into aquifers."[46] In general, waste-disposal methods may not cause an impoundment of water.[47]

AN EVALUATION OF ENVIRONMENTAL CONTROLS

In chapter 4 it was indicated that environmental regulation could be approached in terms of prohibition (of production), prevention (of damage-causing actions), correction (of damages), compensation (for damages), or taxation (of unwanted effects). We argued that where

[40] Ibid., § 11(B)-(G).
[41] Ibid.
[42] Ibid.
[43] Ibid., § 12.
[44] Ibid., § 13.
[45] Ibid., § 14.
[46] Ibid.
[47] Ibid.

environmental costs could be measured as a function of production the best approach was to impose a tax (fee or charge) corresponding to these costs and to allow the operator to choose the profit-maximizing combination of prevention, correction, and so forth, in order to avoid the tax. We now consider the extent to which such an approach may be feasible in outer continental shelf oil and gas operations, coal mining, and oil shale mining and processing.

OUTER CONTINENTAL SHELF OIL AND GAS OPERATIONS

It is clear that the present approach is to rely upon direct prevention (requirements governing well casing, blowout preventers, and storm chokes) and correction (requirement of clean up of oil spills). These requirements are conditioned in no way upon economic considerations, and no effort is made to measure costs and benefits of required actions. There is therefore the possibility that environmental controls impose a cost upon the industry that exceeds the alternative environmental cost, and that oil and gas tend to bear more than their full social costs. This does not necessarily mean that we are made worse off by imposing controls (as against having no controls at all) but only that we might be made better off by a different approach to control.

The matter may be illustrated by figure 8-1. S_pS_p is the supply schedule of the industry in the absence of any effort to internalize externalities; it reflects only internal costs. S_sS_s is the supply schedule reflecting all social costs, external as well as internal. (Assume that an appropriate tax is levied on environmental damage and the operator adopts the profit-maximizing combination of prevention, correction, or compensation.) $S'_pS'_p$ is the supply schedule resulting from controls designed to prevent environmental damages. DD is the demand schedule. With externalities precisely internalized, by means of a tax, for instance, output is Q_s and price is P_s (given by the intersection of DD and S_sS_s). Without internalization effort, output is Q_p and price is P_p, and the welfare loss is the area of triangle ABC. (Incremental social cost along AB is greater than incremental value along AC.) With controls to prevent damages, output is Q'_p and price is P'_p, and the welfare loss is the area of the triangle AGF. (Incremental social cost along GA is less than incremental value along FA.) Since AGF is smaller than ABC, by assumption, we are better off with prevention controls than without any internalizing effort, but worse off than if we could measure environ-

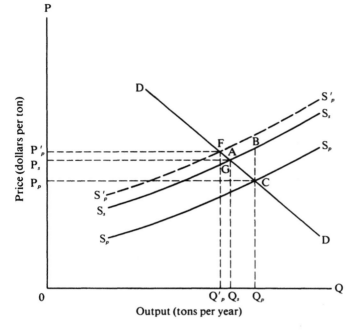

Figure 8-1. Economics of environmental controls.

mental costs and impose a charge on output exactly equal (output Q_s and price P_s). That we are worse off with Q_p' and P_p' than with Q_s and P_s implies that the increment to cost due to controls is greater than the incremental value of environmental protection. Note that we must be able to measure the cost of environmental damage to make such a statement. (Note further that if environmental controls are sufficiently expensive, AGF would be larger than ABC, and we would make ourselves worse off by imposing the controls.)

With this background, let us consider the problem in outer continental shelf oil and gas production.

Well-casing regulations are designed primarily to protect freshwater-bearing strata from invasion by oil or salt water. But to a certain degree they also facilitate oil and gas recovery by keeping unwanted fluids out of the well bore. Thus, their full cost is not assignable exclusively to environmental protection. As for the environmental damages they prevent, measurement (for purposes of taxation or compensation) would only be feasible if monitoring wells were drilled to freshwater-bearing strata at numerous locations and varying distances around oil and gas wells and frequent samples of fresh water were analyzed. This obviously could be very expensive, depending on the number and depths of the relevant strata. There is therefore, in our judgment, a strong likelihood that in most cases the net costs of well-casing requirements are less than those of alternative approaches requiring measurement (taxation or compensation). We cannot say anything regarding the relation of costs to benefits other than that if benefits are small, casing requirements are probably less likely to impose unnecessary costs upon the industry.

Blowout preventers and storm chokes are intended to prevent oil spills; and such spills as occur must be cleaned up at the expense of the lessee. Nothing is known about the probability of oil spills in the absence of preventive devices and effort, or about the distribution by size of damages from such spills as would occur. Therefore, it is not possible to say that preventive measures cost more or less than either the damages they prevent or the costs of correcting such damage as would occur in their absence. With respect to damages that occur despite preventive measures, it is quite possible, but, again, unassertable with certainty, that compensation of those injured would be less expensive than cleanup, at least in some cases.

The basic difficulty with compensation is that negotiations (and perhaps litigation) with injured parties takes time, and the extent of damage from an oil spill is itself a function of time. The longer that control and cleanup are delayed, the greater the potential damage. Thus the very effort to avoid the expense of cleanup may preclude a satisfactory arrangement for compensation and ultimately necessitate cleanup at an enlarged expense. In the absence of good measures of costs and benefits showing the contrary, it is difficult to avoid the conclusion that a combination of preventive measures and requirement of prompt cleanup is the most satisfactory approach to oil spills, even though it may on occasion overcharge the industry's products for environmental costs.

There is another dimension to the problem of oil spills. As noted above, the lessee has an unlimited liability for the expense of cleaning up spills. To a large firm this need not be a major problem, but to a small firm it could mean the difference between survival and bankruptcy. It is possible therefore that unlimited liability tends to repel small bidders in outer continental shelf lease sales and reduce competition accordingly.

We believe this is not a major problem. In the first place, the technology, expense, and general risks of offshore operations impose a substantial size requirement upon participating firms, quite independently of the problem of oil spills and cleanup. In the second place, smaller firms may spread risk by associating themselves with others in joint ventures, including unitized reservoirs. In the third place, preventive measures lower the probability of a major spill and make the likely expense of a given firm rather low. It has been estimated that the notorious Santa Barbara spill of 1969 cost the four companies involved a total of about $10.5 million for oil well-control efforts, oil collection efforts, and beach cleanup.[48] Such an expense occurring once in, say, ten years should be well within the means of a company capable of continuous operations in offshore areas. In the fourth place, insurance by private companies is available to small firms.

One way of looking at preventive measures is to regard them and their expense as insurance premiums. They reduce the probability of losses from liability for oil spills. As such, they encourage entry and competition by relatively small firms and thus indirectly confer a benefit aside from environmental protection. Seen another way, they reduce the cost assignable to environmental protection and make it less likely that oil and gas bear more than their social costs.

Although prevention and correction are theoretically second-best approaches to environmental protection in oil and gas operations on the outer continental shelf, they are accessible and workable; whereas the theoretically best approach—charges for measured damages—is generally not accessible or workable. We accordingly endorse present measures of prevention and correction, not simply as means of environmental protection but as measures tending to assure that the government capture only the true economic rent available from outer continental shelf lands.

COAL-MINING OPERATIONS

Environmental regulations governing coal mining also take the approaches of prevention and correction. Required preventive measures

---

[48] W. J. Mead, "Social Benefit–Cost Analysis of Offshore Drilling," in E. J. Mitchell, ed., *The Question of Offshore Oil* (Washington, D.C., American Enterprise Institute for Public Policy Research, 1976) p. 73, citing W. J. Mead and P. E. Sorensen, "The Economic Cost of the Santa Barbara Oil Spill," *Santa Barbara Oil Symposium,* December 17, 1970, p. 225.

include provision of pillars in underground mines of adequate size to preclude surface subsidence, stabilization of spoil piles to control erosion, plugging of auger holes to prevent harmful drainage or hazards to persons and animals, protection of streams from siltage and poisonous wastes, and the construction of safe impoundments for the disposal of wastes. Following strip mining or comparable disturbance of the surface, corrective measures focus upon the restoration of contours, topsoil, and vegetation.

With regard to preventive procedures, they contemplate alternative damages to persons, animals, and the environment the measurement of which would, in most cases, prove exceedingly expensive or impossible. Consider, for instance, the monitoring effort that would be required over an indefinite period to measure steam damage from toxic drainage, with these measurements to be the basis of compensation or taxation. Consider the required areal extent of such monitoring; and consider the problem of assigning pecuniary values to the damages measured. It seems extremely unlikely that compensation or taxation could be substituted successfully, or at a lower cost, for preventive effort in the relevant cases.

The matter of corrective procedures is different, or may be so in many instances. The principal application is to strip mining, in which the natural surface of the affected land is removed to give access to the coal. At least temporarily, the value of the land for surface uses is destroyed. In many instances, particularly where the land is or may be used for agriculture, grazing, or forestry, the surface value of the land can be meaningfully determined. The destruction of this value is the proper measure of the environmental cost of associated coal mining. This cost is adequately internalized if the coal-mining operation is charged with it and required to pay it to the lessor, or to restore the surface, whichever is cheaper.[49] Note that the operator would opt for restoration whenever its cost was less than the value restored.

Charging the coal operator for the value of land destroyed would have two economic advantages over an unconditional requirement of restoration. First, it would induce the operator to choose the least-cost combination of mining methods, spoil disposal, and either restoration or compensation. (Note that where the value of the land destroyed is charged to coal operations the devices of taxation and compensation

---

[49] It is assumed that mineral rent payments compensate the lessor for lost use of the surface while mining goes on.

coincide.) Second, it would tend to avoid the possibility of imposing on the operator (and society) a greater resource cost than the value of what is restored. In short, it would promote the general economy of productive resources and would incorporate into the cost of coal no more than the actual environmental cost. It would thus tend to result in the capture by the lessor of all the pure economic rent available.

The procedure to be followed in levying the charge might be as follows. The surface value of the land would be estimated (and stipulated in the offer of lease), and as mining proceeded it would be payable in proportion to land disturbance. Thus, if the coal to be mined lay under 100 acres, one one-hundredth of the land value might be paid per acre disturbed. With good foreknowledge of the amount and configuration of the coal deposit, the payment might be translated into a charge per ton removed. In any case, the funds would be held in escrow and would be refunded to the operator if and as the land surface is restored. If the operator should opt for compensation rather than restoration, the funds would become the property of the lessor.

We emphasize that this approach may be feasible in many, but not all, instances. In other instances the problem is that of measuring the value of the land where it is associated primarily with wildlife habitat, scenery, and the like. This is much more difficult than when the land has commercial uses. Another is that of determining whether, or the degree to which, value has been restored. Much land has more than one possible use and it may be restored for some uses but not others. In some cases, as where erosion is a problem and restoration of vegetation dependent on a favorable pattern of rainfall, it may not be possible to determine whether value is, in fact, restored for many years following cessation of mining operations. (Note that this last is also a problem in policing a general restoration requirement.) Another problem is that of defining the affected area of surface land. Mining and disposition of spoil may occupy, say, 100 acres; but ultimately erosion, siltation, and the like may adversely affect many more acres if the 100 acres are not restored. And there may be other problems. In any case, taxation and compensation as an alternative to restoration probably cannot be universally applied.

Where it can be applied it should be, however. Otherwise we run the risk of loading upon coal greater costs than are economically warranted, with attendant sacrifice of resources (coal or labor and capital) and a lesser degree of capture of the pure economic rent available.

OIL SHALE OPERATIONS

In the light of the foregoing we can quickly deal with the problem of environmental costs in oil-shale operations. As with coal mining, the regulations contemplate a combination of prevention and restoration. We can suggest no adequate, economically feasible substitute for the preventive measures required. As for corrective measures, the same considerations apply to the matter of taxation and compensation versus restoration of the surface. However, it is our understanding that the lands thus far affected by leases are valuable primarily for recreation, wildlife, scenery, and the like—rather than for agriculture, grazing, or forestry—so that the determination of surface value would be difficult. Moreover, there is no real experience with large-scale commercial operations, so that it may not be possible to anticipate all the problems of either valuation or restoration that may be encountered. We are left with the uncomfortable conclusion that the lease provisions for preventive and corrective measures in oil shale operations are perhaps the best we can do; but that they may unnecessarily and uneconomically deny us some part of our fuel resources.

CONCLUSION

For the most part we are unable to suggest feasible changes in the present approach to environmental regulation in fossil fuels production. We have, however, attempted to define the problem in a way that may be helpful in future decisions. We should, in any case, bear in mind that the objective is not to protect the environment at any cost and to the exclusion of other objectives, but to properly allocate costs to the minerals we do and may produce. With this objective in view, we should continually seek ways to measure environmental costs so that we can make taxation and compensation as feasible as prevention and correction in environmental regulation.

9

Conclusions and Recommendations

In the leasing of federal lands for minerals production the Department of the Interior seeks three objectives: orderly and timely resource development, environmental protection, and a fair market value for natural resources. We have argued that these objectives may be integrated into a more general rule, and that the department should seek to capture a maximum of the present value of pure economic rent arising from minerals production, where "pure economic rent" is the income which tends to accrue in the long run, under conditions of perfect competition and the absence of externalities, to the owners of natural resources. There are several reasons for this rule. First, it gives a concrete meaning to "orderly and timely" resource development and "fair market value," while recognizing the need to internalize externalities such as environmental damages. Second, it is the equivalent, in effect, to the rule that the Department of the Interior should seek to maximize the (present) value of resources to society. Third, pure economic rent is an economic surplus, the capture of which by the Department of the Interior does not affect output, the price level, or relative prices and the allocation of resources. Fourth, as a form of governmental revenue, economic rent received by the department substitutes for taxes which would affect output, prices, and resource allocation. Thus, following the rule promotes general economic efficiency and tends to maximize the value of resources to society.

Of course, the Interior Department cannot measure pure economic rent a priori and set the price of leases accordingly. Rather, in order to follow the rule it must create conditions conducive to its satisfaction in the normal process of marketing leases. Thus, conditions which reduce uncertainty, increase competition, promote the optimum rate of extraction of minerals, internalize externalities, and relate the rate of leasing to the projected capacity of the affected industries all tend to satisfy the rule. Note that the rule is not the same as that of maximizing the present value of land revenues, for the latter would call for disregarding environmental costs and lead to the exploitation of some minerals whose social cost exceeded their social value.

Of special relevance to the leasing of oil and gas lands is the fact that unregulated competition (within common reservoirs) in oil and gas production tends to result in an inefficient time-distribution of extraction, excessive investment in wells, and an uneconomic loss of ultimate recovery. This result stems from the fact that because of the fugitive nature of the resource the operator who restrains current extraction tends to lose oil or gas to his neighbors in a common reservoir. This, being a private cost to him but not a social cost, leads him (and his competitors) to extract at a rate which is socially inappropriate. It results in a lower private value of leases than social value and the capture by the landowner of less than the pure economic rent available. Thus the system of regulation of oil and gas operations by the Geological Survey has the potential for increasing the proportion of pure economic rent captured in competitive leases by the Department of the Interior.

These conceptual and theoretical considerations lead to certain practical conclusions. With regard to the manner of leasing, we conclude that all leases of federal lands should be by competitive bidding. More specifically, competitive bidding should be substituted for the lottery system of awarding oil and gas leases of onshore lands not located on a known geological structure. The Department of the Interior cannot hope to capture the full economic rent from such lands if potential lessees are not required to compete for them. As for oral versus sealed bids, we conclude that under the condition of uncertainty, which is characteristic of mineral leasing, especially with respect to oil and gas, sealed bids are more likely to yield rents approximating pure economic rent and are, therefore, to be preferred.

The rate of leasing (for example, on the outer continental shelf) affects the present value of pure economic rent in two opposing ways. Speeding up the receipt of given rents tends to increase present value. Speeding up the offer of leases tends to depress the rents offered, primarily because of increased uncertainty and rising marginal costs of operations constrained by lease terms. These considerations suggest an optimum rate of leasing, but we are unable to specify what this is in precise quantitative terms. Of particular relevance to rising marginal costs of operations is the capacity of the industries supplying inputs to mineral operators. Marginal costs would not rise so steeply if supply industries could with certainty anticipate the rate of leasing, know how long the rate would be sustained, and were given time by means of a slow increase in the rate to adjust capacity. We suggest, accordingly, that leasing could with benefit be accelerated if the buildup were gradual, if the new higher rate ultimately to be achieved were known in advance, and if, in the light of the total area ultimately to be leased, the new rate could be sustained for a long enough period of time to justify additional capacity in the supply industries. The recent, very sharp increase in the rate of leasing of outer continental shelf lands seems not well calculated to conform to these conditions and therefore to increase unambiguously the present value of expected economic rent.

Given the desirability of competitive bidding for leases, there are many possible bases of bidding, the principal ones of which we have considered. Bonus bidding has the advantage of leading to a lump-sum front-end payment which does not affect subsequent exploration, development, and production decisions. (It does not affect the margin of exploitation.) It has the disadvantage of requiring substantial operator capital and settling the full burden of risk or uncertainty on the lessee. (It tends to restrain competition and increase discount rates.) Royalty bidding has generally opposite effects. It tends to alter the margin of exploitation, but minimizes uncertainty and capital requirements. Experimental evidence indicates that it increases competition but leads to such high royalty percentages as seriously to contract the margin of exploitation. Profit-share bidding is similar in effect to royalty bidding, but with somewhat less adverse effect on the margin of exploitation. Its major disadvantage is the necessity for the lessor to monitor the financial records of the lessee. These considerations lead us to conclude that a system of bonus bidding with a modest fixed royalty, as is now the practice, is probably to be preferred.

As for variations on the bonus-bidding system, we conclude that joint bidding by all but the largest bidders should be allowed as tending, on balance, to increase competition; and that sequential bidding, installment bonus payment, and working-interest bidding should be experimented with in order to gain greater insights into their effects. We see little to gain from decreasing tract size on the outer continental shelf. We reject as unsound—that is, as tending to induce uneconomic expenditures for exploration and development—the Halbouty plan of a credit against a bonus for exploration and development expenditures. We also reject contract exploration financed by the Department of the Interior, largely on the grounds that "exploration" is not sharply distinguishable from "development," so that the extent of the department's direction and financing cannot be precisely defined a priori.

On the matter of regulation of oil and gas operations by the Geological Survey, particularly on the outer continental shelf, we conclude that the Geological Survey should require unitization of reservoirs and otherwise leave well spacing, production plans, and production rates to be chosen freely by lessee-operators. Unitization—the pooling of separate properties in a common reservoir, the sharing of costs and revenues by prearranged formula, and the operation of the reservoir as a single unit—directly attacks the problem of discrepancy between private and social costs leading to excessive rates of output, and so forth, in oil and gas operations. It makes it impossible for one operator to gain oil or gas at the expense of a neighbor. As a direct and complete solution of the basic problem, it is superior to regulation based on the MER, even when the MER is defined with economic content and particularly when it is not. At best, the MER is a partial solution; and at worst, it reduces capturable rent (and value to society) by emphasizing physical recovery to the exclusion of efficiency in the use of all economic resources.

Environmental regulation plays a legitimate role in the matter of maximizing the capture of available pure economic rent. The objective, however, should not be to protect the environment from alteration, but to internalize environmental costs so that minerals extraction bears its full social costs, no more and no less. Internalization may be approached in terms of prohibition (of production), prevention (of damage-causing actions), correction (of damages), compensation (for damages), or taxation (of unwanted effects). In general, where environmental damages can be measured in pecuniary terms, taxation (charges or fees) at rates corresponding to these damages is to be preferred, with the operator free to choose the profit-maximizing combination of abstinence, prevention, correction, and compensation in order to avoid the tax. This tends to internalize costs in the most efficient way. However, the problems of measuring and monitoring environmental damages in minerals extraction are so varied and difficult that, generally, a second-best approach of prevention and correction must be accepted. Perhaps only in the case of strip-mining on lands with commercial value is the "ideal" approach of charges for damages practically accessible.

What changes in the law would be required to effect these specific recommendations? First, in order to make competitive sales of mineral leases universal it would be necessary to change that section of the Mineral Leasing Act which mandates the granting of oil and gas leases on lands not overlying a known geological structure to the first qualified applicant.[1] Second, although the matter is not entirely clear, it would perhaps require amendments to the Mineral Leasing Act and the Outer Continental Shelf Lands Act to enable installment-bonus payment and working-interest bidding for oil and gas leases, which we recommend on an experimental basis. Finally, the law would have to be changed to permit the preferred approach to environmental controls: taxation, with operator freedom to choose the profit-maximizing combination of prevention, correction, and compensation. The law would *not* have to be changed in order to permit universal sealed bidding where competitive leasing is authorized, to permit the acceleration of leasing of mineral lands, particularly oil and gas lands in the outer continental shelf, to permit bonus bidding with adjustable royalty rate specified, to permit joint and sequential bidding, or to require unitization of oil and gas reservoirs and the formation of "logical mining units" in coal. In general, then, our recommendations would require few changes in the law, but a number of changes in operating regulations.

It may be noted here that proposed 1977 amendments to the Outer Continental Shelf Lands Act, passed by the Senate,[2] but not by the House, would have permitted bonus bidding, royalty bidding (both now allowed), profit-share bidding, work-commitment bidding, and other systems proposed by the secretary and not specifically disapproved by the Congress.[3] The amendments would have restricted bonus bidding to no more than 50 percent of leased area in new provinces.[4] They would have permitted deferred payment of cash bonuses.[5] Similar legislation is pending in the Congress as this is written (July 1978).

There is one remaining problem, mentioned earlier but deserving of some emphasis here. Many federal lands that are actually or potentially

---

[1] 30 U.S.C. 226(a)-(d).
[2] S. 9, July 15, 1977.
[3] Sec. 205(a).
[4] Sec. 205(a)(8).
[5] Sec. 205(a)(4).

productive of minerals lie adjacent to state and private lands, and often the federal government owns only mineral rights, surface rights having been sold to nonfederal interests. Where actual or potential mineral deposits overlap federal-state or federal-private interfaces, or where mineral and surface rights are separately owned, special problems of regulation arise. In general, the federal jurisdiction is confined to federal properties and state jurisdiction applies to other properties. The states differ in the kinds and degrees of regulation imposed in their respective jurisdictions. Historically, the federal authorities have largely yielded to the states when regulations differ and a conflict is involved. For example, oil production regulations on federal lands in the public domain largely imitate or conform with state regulations. Until 1970 the market-demand prorationing practices of Louisiana and Texas were extended to the Gulf outer continental shelf. In encouraging oil reservoir unitization the federal authorities have been less than free in some instances where reservoirs overlap federal and state or private lands. Thus, given this tradition, federal authorities may not be able to follow our suggestions even if they were disposed to do so. We do not know the solution to this problem, but note it here as a limitation on the applicability of our recommendations.

Although we have not been able to suggest practical solutions to all the problems associated with the leasing of federal lands for minerals production, we have shown, it is hoped, that an approach based on the rule of maximizing the capture of the present value of pure economic rent is a valid and fruitful one. Aside from working out some of the major implications of this rule, we have shown the proper role of regulation, with respect to both production rates and environmental protection, in association with federal land leasing. Perhaps these contributions justify the effort.

Index